To
present and former residents
of the House of Affirmation
with love and gratitude

Published with Ecclesiastical Permission

First Edition
© 1983 by House of Affirmation, Inc.

Library of Congress Cataloging in Publication Data
Psychotheological Symposium, 8th, 1982, Fontbonne Academy, etc.
    Relationships: issues of emotional living in an age of stress for clergy and religious.
        1. Catholic Church—Clergy—Psychology—Congresses.
2. Monastic and religious life—Psychology—Congresses.
I. Helldorfer, Martin C.   II. Sammon, Sean D., 1947-
III. Title.
    BX1912.7.P78   1982   253′.2   83-2706

ISBN 0-89571-015-3

Printed by
Mercantile Printing Company, Worcester, Massachusetts
United States of America

RELATIONSHIPS

ISSUES OF EMOTIONAL LIVING
IN AN AGE OF STRESS
FOR CLERGY AND RELIGIOUS

THE EIGHTH
PSYCHOTHEOLOGICAL SYMPOSIUM

MARTIN C. HELLDORFER

ANNA POLCINO

NEIL RYAN CASTRONOVO

THOMAS A. KANE

AUDREY E. CAMPBELL-WRAY

JOHN A. STRUZZO

GONG SHU

KATHLEEN E. KELLEY

MARIE R. HOFER

EDITED BY SEAN D. SAMMON

AFFIRMATION BOOKS
WHITINSVILLE, MASSACHUSETTS

All income derived from the sale of this book is used by the House of Affirmation to provide care for priests and religious suffering from emotional unrest.

AFFIRMATION BOOKS is an important part of the ministry of the House of Affirmation, International Therapeutic Center for Clergy and Religious, founded by Sister Anna Polcino, S.C.M.M., M.D. House of Affirmation centers are located in Boston, Hopedale, and Whitinsville, Massachusetts; Webster Groves, Missouri; Montara, California; and Knowle, England.

CONTENTS

Foreword

The complexity of human living testifies that there is no simple recipe for happiness. However, poets, songwriters, philosophers, and theologians, as well as the immediate experience of every human being, point to one necessary ingredient: some kind of intimate relationship. *Relationship* is what life is all about: relationship with one's world, self, others, and God.

Christianity is all about relationship. Its essential teaching is that respectful intimacy with one's friend, neighbor, God, and the world brings happiness "in this world and the next." In fact, so important is relationship in Christian theology that it teaches that the love relationship of the Father for the Son and the Son for the Father results in a person—Love—whom we call the Holy Spirit.

Affirmation is all about relationship. The essays in this book, *Relationships: Issues of Emotional Living in an Age of Stress for Clergy and Religious,* are the brief reflections of a few of our House of Affirmation staff members. Their observations are not meant to be complete in themselves, but to encourage the reader to further thought and discussion.

Affirmation Books is happy to bring this volume to the reading public. While we have tried to keep printing and production costs low, I regret that this book represents a significant increase in price. I hope that the income from these publications will keep our books viable and a significant contribution to the dialogue between psychology and theology.

Brother Sean D. Sammon, F.M.S., Ph.D., the editor of this volume, is a special gift of God to the House of Affirmation ministry. While Brother Sean's clinical and academic abilities have brought him international acclaim, his colleagues know that it is his relationship with Jesus and His Church that makes Brother Sean the person he is: a compelling religious whose healing words of affirmation effect lasting good.

Thomas A. Kane, Ph.D., D.P.S.
Priest, Diocese of Worcester
Publisher, Affirmation Books
Whitinsville, Massachusetts

10 January 1983

Preface

A genuine relationship heralds some good and bad news! First, the good news. A relationship's rewards are great. The bad news? Building one is hard work. Does any of this news come as a surprise? Probably not. Most men and women know that genuine relationships have their "ups-and-downs." Demanding patience, loyalty, enthusiasm, and communication, they also make people less selfish. Forming relationships is a lot of work but the rewards are tremendous: a rare tenderness, surprise on a daily basis, transformation.

Not easy to come by, a genuine relationship is also not due solely to chance. People are not born with the ability to form genuine relationships. Rather, they learn to build them. In accepting this challenge they forget about propriety. They take a chance, make mistakes, try again. Needless to say, men and women need a healthy supply of self-esteem for the work.

Furthermore, unless you love yourself, chances are you will fall short in your attempts to love anybody else. Part of the problem is this: why believe that another can love you if you do not love yourself? Feeling unlovable, some men and women continually test their relationships. No matter what others do to show them they care, it is never enough. In trying to force others, even God, to *prove* their love, these people ultimately lose. Their approach just does not work because they have not learned to receive love, particularly their own.

The eighth annual House of Affirmation symposium examined the topic of relationships. The present volume, *Relationships: Issues of Emotional Living in an Age of Stress for Clergy and Religious,* offers the provocative essays presented at the symposium by my House of Affirmation colleagues. From a variety of standpoints, they address many important areas: relationships and the nonverbal language of emotions; the importance of solitude and human relationships in building a relationship with God; creativity in one's relationships; the paradox of relating to one's shadow and also finding a gem; maturity in intimate relationships, both heterosexual and homosexual; necessary ingredients for living out the Christian call to be full of love; the meaning of celibate renunciation for the awkward, proclaiming, and "grumpy" children of God; relationships and the language of our bodies; the challenge of living celibately while also being in love with another person. We present these essays proudly for your reading, reflection, and discussion.

I am grateful to those speakers who presented papers at the Boston, Louisville, San Francisco, and Saint Louis 1982 symposium sessions. At the same time, in the name of our staff I thank the men and women who attended these sessions. Each year the participants are both a challenge to our thinking and a support for our work. We rely on them to join us as we explore together important areas in the lives of today's religious professionals.

Many friends and staff members devoted their time and energies to planning and executing the symposium's activities: to each and all, a sincere thank-you. The symposium moderators deserve special mention for handling the many organizational details that made the days run smoothly: Dr. E. J. Franasiak (Boston); Sister Geraldine Marie Heavrin, S.C.N. (Louisville); Sister Kathleen Kelley, S.N.D. (Saint Louis); Sister Patricia Hauser, S.P. (San Francisco).

We are also grateful to those who extended hospitality for the meetings: the Sisters of Saint Joseph at Fontbonne Academy in Milton, Massachusetts; the Sisters of the Presentation in San Francisco; and the staff at Saint John's Mercy Hospital in Saint

Louis. This year for the first time we brought the symposium to Louisville, Kentucky. We are grateful to our cosponsors there: the Senate of Religious, Senate of Priests, and Continuing Education for Clergy.

At each House of Affirmation center, the symposium is part of our annual Affirmation Weekend. At this time each year, many of our former residents return to renew their friendships and celebrate the personal journey they have undertaken. It is a time to rejoice! The return of these men and women also encourages the staff and present residents in the work they have undertaken together. We are thankful for the men and women, past and present, who have come aside to the House of Affirmation. Their inspiration is the source of many things great and beautiful.

> Sean D. Sammon, F.M.S.
> House of Affirmation

2 January 1983 Whitinsville, Massachusetts

Brother Martin C. Helldorfer, F.S.C., D.Min., assistant director and full-time psychotherapist at the Boston-Hopedale House of Affirmation, is a Christian Brother. He holds degrees in theology, chemistry, and religion and personality, and received his doctorate from Andover Newton Theological School. Brother Helldorfer is the author of *The Work Trap* and a frequent contributor to religious journals and periodicals.

Love: A Need, A Gift, and A Taboo

Martin C. Helldorfer

It's by far the hardest thing I've ever done:
To be so in love with you and so alone.

—John Denver

Our Need for Rosarys

The topic of this chapter is the rightness of and the need for intimate, loving heterosexual relationships among the Church's ministers. Perhaps the following story is the best way to introduce this topic:

A parish in the wilds of northern Alaska was so isolated that the bishop consistently had trouble finding a priest to minister to it. It was no secret that in one year, six of the seven men invited to take the parish declined to do so. The man who eventually agreed to go was a saintly fellow well-known for his generosity and selfless ways. Needless to say, the bishop was appreciative and promised—as a kind of favor—that he would personally visit the priest each year and would also provide the money for his return home whenever he felt a need to do so.

As it happened the priest did not return home often, and the bishop did not visit yearly. In fact, it was four years before the latter traveled north to administer the sacrament of confirmation. When the two men met, the bishop was quick to thank the priest for his dedication and service to the people of that remote region of the diocese.

"I only wish I had more men like you," he told the pastor. "But tell me, how is it that you can stay here so peacefully when others find the assignment so difficult? What is your secret?"

"Well, your Excellency, I must admit that I couldn't do this without my Rosary and my Martini."

The bishop was impressed. Here was a man of simplicity. His needs were few, and his reliance on prayer was encouraging.

"That reminds me," the pastor added. "I forgot to ask if you would enjoy a Martini before dinner."

"Certainly," the bishop replied.

It was then that the pastor turned in his chair and said, "Rosary, make it two!"

Now you know the kind of relationship that I have in mind. I am going to speak of our need for Rosarys.

No, I am not going to discuss our need for lovers. Neither am I going to try to develop an apologia for romantic love. I will speak about our need for relationships that resemble the taken-for-granted, not-so-romantic connectedness that develops between a husband and wife over the years. To my knowledge there is no popularly-used word to describe such love. The nearest we come to it is when we speak of married couples who have become friends.

I have no statistical evidence to substantiate the existence or frequency of such love among celibate persons, but I do know that such relationships exist. In this essay I want to speak to those who know such love. I want to encourage them because I am certain that it is difficult to love as they do and yet live as priests, sisters, or brothers.

I have still another interest in addressing the topic. Men and women who love as intimate friends in this way are gifts to all of us. I have lost count of the number of persons with whom I have spoken in the past months who experience a split between the love of another and their vocation as a sister, priest, or brother. Today we are in special need of those men and women who can teach us how to combine the two.

Relationships of Care

First it is necessary to clarify what I mean by intimate hetero-sexual love. I am referring to relationships of care that have grown over the years. These relationships have endured the first flush of emotion, have passed through stages of infatuation, and have bonded two persons in a way as intangible as it is unde-niable. Anne Morrow Lindbergh's phrase "the mingling of two solitudes," which she uses to describe the marriage relationship, is an apt way to characterize the love to which I refer.

When speaking of an intimate, loving relationship among celi-bates I am not referring to a relationship that is one among many. I am referring to a kind of love relationship that is as pro-tected and nourished as any marital love.

Relationships develop in varied ways, yet there is often a pat-tern. First, care is awakened. Then bonds of concern and affec-tion develop. As years pass, the two lives become intermingled. Frequently the love develops almost imperceptibly as the man and woman work together. If they were married, the process would be manifest in the creation of a home and family. The bonds for celibate persons may form in working on shared proj-ects. Married or unmarried, a feeling of communion awakens. There is nothing otherworldly or particularly romantic about the way love grows; it all takes place in the humdrum of everyday life.

With time the two persons grow familiar with each other. Not only is the world that is being built a shared activity, but it also includes a kind of at-homeness with the other. They grow to care increasingly for each other, and they move toward expressing that care in bodily ways. Signs of affection occur spontaneously. They become as comfortable with the other's hand and body as with their own. Letting down their guardedness with each other is as pleasurable as it is indicative of a relaxedness with each other in every area of their lives.

Obviously, this kind of love is built over years. In a manner of speaking the relationship is exclusive but, like marital love at its best, it is a love that is turned outward toward others. Freedom, rather than constraint, is its characteristic.

Hidden Relationships

At first, I thought that kind of love was unknown among celibate persons. We do not usually see such relationships in the give and take of everyday life. Psychotherapists see many people who are involved with others in a way that may be described as intimate, but there is usually a troublesome aspect to the relationships. For one reason or another, the love I am referring to is hidden from the view of curious eyes.

However, the recognition of intimate love between celibate persons is not a recent phenomenon. Recall the lives of Teresa and John, Francis de Sales and Jeanne de Chantal, Clare and Francis—to mention the sainted—and we have reason to be assured that our topic is not a forbidden one. Each of those couples knew about love of another human being. No one will easily convince me that these saints were able to write of God's love without first knowing the intimacy of another person. Read the poetry of Pope John Paul II. Look behind the lines and conjecture about his life. I think you will find that we have a pope who knows of human love. But why is it that we hear so little of such love? Why is it kept from sight?

Fear of criticism is one factor. We live in a culture that eroticizes relationships, and few persons are willing to open themselves to the suspicion that their love is a forbidden one. At the same time those men and women who are involved in caring relationships are unwilling to forfeit what is life giving for them. As a consequence, the relationship is kept from sight.

In addition, there is the widespread belief that the intimate love of another will hinder the investment that a person is able to make in the community or diocese. After all, one who loves another individual may not be totally given to the community and its interests. Wanting to avoid such criticism, those who love will be inclined to keep their affections hidden.

There are other reasons. Perhaps those who have grown close to each other know what a gift their love is. They may realize that others crave the same gift but are unable to find it. Thus, their sensitivity may lead them to keep their love hidden from view.

Neither would I rule out self-protecting motives, such as the desire to avoid the jealousy or resentment of others. Nor would I overlook the fact that those who love might soon feel alienated if their love were revealed. I know a priest who says that he would never let anyone know that he has loved someone for years. "My parishioners would lynch me if they knew. Each person believes that I am there for them whenever needed. If they thought I was close to someone, they would resent it. Being a priest in this parish means having no close relationships—at least none that are known."

Whether understandable or not, it is tragic to drive relationships underground. Mushrooms live well in the dark; people do not. When we have to live in hiding, distortions develop. Suppose a person's mother or father dies. Suppose, too, that the atmosphere of the rectory or community in which that person lives is such that feelings cannot be expressed. We know how dangerous that situation is for the people involved. To live in an atmosphere where we are unable to share our feelings of love and affection is just as dangerous.

Having to keep our relationships hidden causes more problems than it solves. Life that has to be lived underground is subject to distortion because it lacks the give and take that contact with others provides. We all know the more or less unusual instance of the priest who is a well-liked and effective minister and who is later discovered to be married and the father of a family. We seem surprised that a person could live such a double life. I am sure that such an example is unusual, but it does portray what can happen to those who feel that they must keep the love of others from sight. They live two lives, each pulling in a different direction.

When relationships of love go underground, perspective is also lost. Two persons turned toward each other in darkness lose their balance. Carl Jung has written persuasively of the way that the darkened sides of our personalities influence relationships. There is no need to catalog the difficulties. The wise person observes them, the confessor forgives, and the counselor tries to help.

Not only is perspective lost, but sexuality becomes a difficulty. Hidden relationships tend to become eroticized. Thus, relationships that are difficult enough to handle in the light become especially troublesome in the dark.

Lastly, once the hidden love is eroticized, a dichotomy is set up that pits the love relationship against the celibate way of life. An either/or situation is created. Pulled in two seemingly opposed directions, the person feels he or she must choose one or the other. Once the relationship is underground, it is difficult to recognize that love and celibacy go hand in hand.

Perhaps what is most tragic about driving intimate, loving relationships from sight is that we deprive ourselves of the opportunity to learn how to live in the tension that arises whenever life's circumstances take us in one direction and our heart's desires pull in another. This kind of tension is known to the man who chooses to be a priest but whose heart now leads him toward marriage. The married man with a family, feeling the first stirrings of affection for another woman, knows the tension to which I refer. Most of us at some time in our lives will experience such a tension. Some of us live with it almost daily. Celibate persons who love each other intimately can teach us how to live in the tension. That lesson is a gift all of us need.

I have heard it said that talk of such relationships is just one more manifestation of the way that the Church's ministers have become more concerned about themselves than those they serve. I do not agree. The question of loving relationships among the Church's ministers is a critical one. After fourteen years in formation work with young men and women, what stands out in my memory is the fact that so few persons in today's world even consider our way of life as a possibility for them. Our life style is generally thought of as a repressive one. Who wants to live and not love? If the young never see chaste persons who intimately love others, how will they know that it is possible? If we do not slowly work on freeing ourselves to live and love in the light of day we not only do a disservice to ourselves but to others as well.

The Crux: A Change in Spirituality

I have outlined some of the dynamics involved in driving relationships from sight. Another question needs to be asked: why are such relationships rising today? What is happening to us that is bringing about this change? No more than twenty years ago, intimate relationships of love between celibates were not only unseen but often devalued. Today they are valued although still unseen. Why is there such a change?

We are living in a time of unique transition. One spirituality has died and another is being born. To understand the extraordinary repercussions of this transition and its effect on our lives, specifically our relationships with one another, we need to consider the history of spirituality within orders and congregations.

In the early centuries after Christ, many men and a few women flocked to the desert in order to find God. Over the years they developed a characteristic spirituality. It was not long before the popularity of this life style waned, and persons began to group themselves in monasteries. They found God within the monastery, alone but beside one another. In living by the Rule and obeying the abbot they were assured that they were doing God's will. Not many centuries later the canons began to gather around the cathedrals and the monks' way of life decreased in popularity. Just as the monks had developed their spirituality, so did the canons. They took some of the practices of the hermits and monks and changed them to fit the feudal world of lords and kings. Then when walled towns arose, the mendicants appeared. They roamed the streets of those towns and stressed the importance of their presence among the poor rather than set apart in the cloister. They, too, developed a characteristic spirituality. With Ignatius, contemporary service groups came into being. Such groups had a task to do and set out to accomplish it. Missionaries were sent worldwide, schools were opened, and hospitals established. Numerous groups formed to spread the Gospel around the globe. A fifth spirituality developed which we might call a spirituality of service. This spirituality is the one we were living not so long ago.

The rise and decline of the differing spiritualities can be illustrated in the following way:

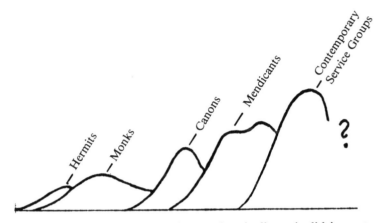

Today, our world is changing as drastically as it did in past centuries when one spirituality gave way to another in a time of transition. We are living in a period when one spirituality has died and another is being born. We can grasp an insight into this phenomenon when we note some of the characteristics of the spirituality that has recently died.

In our beginning years in the seminary or novitiate the spirituality that we lived was one ruled by the clock. Silence was a value; uniformity was stressed; singularity was a fault. We performed "exercises" through which we nourished our spiritual lives. At all costs we were to forget ourselves, and find God in service to those in need.

Fewer and fewer persons live that kind of spirituality today. Think of the men and women religious you know. Did they rise at 5:45 a.m. yesterday? Did they then go to chapel for morning prayer, followed by thirty minutes of mental prayer, Mass, and then breakfast? Chances are they did not. It is also likely that they did not go back to the chapel at noon in order to make their particular examen or to reflect on whether they were faithful to the resolutions they had made during the morning meditation.

Did the persons with whom you live return from their day's activities at 5:00 p.m. in order to make spiritual readings and mental prayer? Did they say night prayer at 9:00 p.m., and then faithfully observe the grand silence last night? Comparing how we lived not so long ago with the way we live today, we can see how profoundly our spirituality has changed.

One pervading characteristic of that past spirituality was its stress on aloneness. Often enough, that stress became an emphasis on isolation. At its best, this spirituality bred individuals; at its worst, it forced some men and women into isolation. Those were the years that we feared particular friendships, and lived with a spoken and unspoken fear of contact with persons of the opposite sex. As a result of this spirituality most of us had few relationships outside—and sometimes inside—our communities.

Spirituality of Today

Today, the spirituality that we live is hardly a codified one. Instead of uniformity, diversity is valued. The rhythm of our days is no longer that of the twenty-four-hour clock. An exercise approach to life has largely disappeared. Spontaneity is encouraged. One Rule lived in one manner has given way to varying life styles that reflect differences in age, temperament, culture, and ministry. We value relationships, not isolation. If we were at one time advised against contact with others, today the message has changed. Our theologies are relational ones.

We are living in a vastly different world from the one we lived in no more than twenty years ago. In a time of unique change, we are in the process of developing a new spirituality. What is happening between men and women reflects the spirituality that is forming. As uncomfortable as we may feel, we are being thrown toward one another. We must recognize, however, that the relationships that seem so bothersome to us today are not distortions of life so much as they are indications of new life.

Many of us fear what is happening to and around us. We may be afraid of the relationships toward which we are propelled. It is appropriate to approach relationships with fear and trembling, and some of our hesitancies are well-founded. At the same time many of our fears are not. Sometimes we fear the type of relationship I have been discussing simply because we stand outside of it. If you recall, the god Zeus gave Pandora a box from which all human ills escaped when she opened it. Today, we carry such a box. Only the angels, and maybe the devils, know what will happen if we open it. Like Pandora, we both fear and desire what lies within.

Many of us fear that if the box is opened, we will surely lose our vocation. What man living alone in a small room, knowing the frustrations of his ministry, will remain faithful to his commitment in the face of an awakened love for a woman? What woman in a position of leadership within a group whose average age is fifty-six and which has had few novices in recent years will want to continue to live as a sister if she loves another intimately?

Some of us fear that if such relationships develop, we will become genitally involved. However, intimate love does not necessarily move in this direction. The example of Regine Olsen and Soren Kierkegaard is well-known. Soren fell deeply in love with Regine. Not only was he in love, but his engagement symbolized for him the possibility of a normal life. (You may recall that Soren was melancholic and suffered severely from depression). Yet as he grew closer to Regine, he saw that the relationship could not lead to marriage as he desired. The details of how he reached that realization need not concern us here. We need only note that their deepening love led them back into their lives as unmarried individuals and not toward the marriage they desired.

We have no idea where relationships will lead. If we are open to the mystery of life and strive to be persons of integrity, we do well to note our fears but we are also well-advised to face them. Looking at a box from the outside is much different from jumping into it and taking a look around its interior. Again, ask any married couple who knows what it means to speak of marriage as a mingling of solitudes, and you will probably find persons who are able to speak of the difference between looking at a relationship of love from a distance and from within. Ask two celibate persons who have grown to love each other respectfully and intimately and they, too, will be able to speak of how different an intimate relationship appears from within. Many of our fears concerning relationships arise simply from the fact that we stand apart from them.

Facing the changed and changing world in which we live, and knowing something of our need for relationships, how can we help ourselves? Perhaps we should try to formulate practical suggestions to face the problem in a no-nonsense way. Maybe we should talk of how to change the atmosphere of our rectories and communities so that our lives are lived more openly. Or, possibly we should start to look at structures that could facilitate new life within the ministry. Perhaps all of these things need to be done. However, I would like to settle for saying a few words about developing two attitudes that might be of special help to us in the contemporary world. I mention them in all seriousness, but playfully as well.

In Praise of Sin

Sin is not so bad! Maybe we need to speak a word in its defense. The story of Adam and Eve from the Hebrew Scriptures illustrates my point. Before the Fall, our parents blissfully walked the earth. They were not aware that they were naked until they sinned. Sin was the door through which they passed as awareness was awakened. For ages we have called that sin a *felix culpa*. Now think back over your own life experience. We seem to learn—to awaken—in times of conflict and trespassed boundaries. We do not learn very much in times of tranquility. Sin is the road to awareness. Maybe we ministers need a little more of this kind of sin among us.

However, that said, it is also important to note that we do not learn when we deliberately set out to trespass. Such an attitude generally gets us nowhere. The kind of sin I am speaking of comes as a surprise. It is an unexpected development, a blow from the side that hurts. When we open the box of relationships with others, we are opening ourselves to sin. Like that of Adam and Eve the transgression may not be a planned one. It may not even be the one we fear. Nevertheless, it is risky business to open the box; but it is also something of a necessity. We can help ourselves and others by realizing that such sin is not the end of everything. It is the path of awakening and deepening as well as responsibility.

In Praise of Ordinariness

We would also do well to speak of the value of being ordinary. Again, we must be careful to clarify what we mean. As ministers, many of us are not only dutiful and desirous to do good, but also highly idealistic. We read of the saints and strive to live accordingly. We ponder the Scripture stories and try to make them our own. For instance, we read in Paul how the early Christians loved one another and then measure ourselves against the ideal community. We read of Paul's conversion and his resulting life of intimacy with Christ, then strive for that same union. We forget that he was writing at the end of his journey, and overlook the years of searching that preceded his ability to formulate his vision. By comparison, we falter. I wonder if we are not doing ourselves a disservice by such a comparison. Maybe we would help ourselves by realizing that we are still on our journey, that we have hardly begun. It is all right to be ordinary. Furthermore, it may even be necessary if we are to remain faithful to God's designs. Knowing how ordinary we are, perhaps we will grow first to tolerate and then to appreciate the way God is speaking to us in our struggle to become faithful and loving toward one another. If the ideal keeps escaping us, maybe we are looking in the wrong direction for the God who loves us.

Results

Suppose we risk opening Pandora's box, accepting the value of sin, and settling for finding God in the here and now. What can we expect?

First, more intimate loving relationships will probably see the light of day. They will not usher in a new era, and earth will not become heaven. However, we will discover that it is not only possible but valuable to love intimately and respectfully. Some men and women will be gifted with such relationships. All of us will see them more clearly.

What else can we expect?

A Growing Relaxedness

We can expect a degree of relaxedness to appear among us. Those persons who are gifted with such relationships are certain to experience a relief. No longer will they have to hide a relationship they cherish, and they will be able to let down their defenses a little. Those of us without such relationships will probably grow less anxious when we see them simply because we will have observed their value at first hand. Today such relationships make us anxious because they are unseen but hauntingly present. When we are ill and yet not aware of the cause of our sickness, we are troubled. Once we know the illness, even when it is a serious one, we are more relaxed. Relationships are not illnesses, but we fear them. If they are exposed to the light of day, some of our anxiousness surrounding them will be diminished.

Fewer Distortions

We can expect another development. Once loving relationships among celibates are allowed to surface, those relationships will be chastened; for in the light of day, the relationship is no longer the private domain of two persons turned toward each other. The relationship will be tested by life. Chance remarks, unfair evaluations, welcome affirmation, the jealousy of some, and the support of others will all play a part in shaping the love. With such critique and visibility honest love will endure and deepen. Imitations of love and intimacy will be exposed. The critique of everyday life and the chafing that results from contact with others will not only deepen the love but be a guide to the persons involved.

Increasing Support

Relationships are often kept hidden for fear that the persons involved will be rejected. I remember speaking to a particularly sensitive woman, quite articulate and very attractive. In a group discussion about relationships within a community setting—I was the only man and the only outsider to the community—a sister admitted to the other sisters that she loved two persons. She blushed when she told them. Another asked her if it would help her to say who the men were. "Never," she said. "I couldn't do that if the pope asked me." The members of the group were very respectful and did not push her in any way. After the discussion the sister lingered and eventually spoke to me about her experience in the group. Why do you think she was hesitant to reveal the names of the men she loved? Was it to protect them? Did she think others were prying? No. She said the only reason was that she would not have been able to stand it if someone had laughed. Maybe her fears were well-grounded and her hesitancy to reveal herself was wise. My own feeling is that we will take a few jolts when we live outwardly and honestly. But along with the jolts we will find appreciably more support than we imagine. This is especially the case in today's Church. We do have to be prudent in what we say and what we reveal, but if we err today it is on the side of secrecy. That is unfortunate because we then cut ourselves off from a support that we need.

A Growing Sense of Celebration

There is another surprise that awaits us when we let relationships of love surface. We can celebrate. Love yearns to be shared. Notice how young couples in love are quick to tell everyone. "Rejoice with us," they say in so many differing ways. "We have a gift and we want you to know about it." Notice how most of us respond to feelings of affection and love. We hide them and are careful not to let anyone know what goes on within us. Watchfulness is the order of the day. Besides being a curious way to handle such feelings, it is also unfortunate. Love that is acknowledged and relationships that are lived openly can be celebrated. What do I mean by "celebrated"? Merely the ability to say publicly, "Yes, I do love that person." Again, I want to stress that I am not speaking of sentimentality, flamboyancy, or emotional entanglements that are only caricatures of relationships. The chance to celebrate is a gift that we sorely need in today's Church.

An Emerging Freedom

Finally, we can expect one other development. The guardedness that arises when we find ourselves trying to hide will be lifted. Freedom will probably follow. Can you imagine what would happen if more and more of the Church's ministers found themselves feeling free, rather than restrained? You may say that this will never happen, that I am too idealistic, that I am talking to myself. Maybe, but I do not think so. Have you ever lived with a person who is free? Live with such a person long enough and your own heart will be touched. Such men and women have a way of freeing others by their presence. In contrast, have you ever lived with someone who is always and everywhere on guard? Attitudes are contagious. I remember reading that Jung once advised a beginning therapist to get his own house in order before working with others. "Illness is contagious," he used to say. Psychological illnesses are as catching as the common cold. Jung's advice to those he trained is good counsel for the Church's ministers. If we live underground and by constraint, what kind of ministers will we be? We would do well to do some soul-searching to see if we need to change the way we live, the way we force ourselves and others underground. It is a question of justice.

I began these reflections with the words John Denver made famous: "It's by far the hardest thing I've ever done: to be so in love with you and so alone." Relationships, no matter how intimate, lead us toward recognizing our solitude. Anyone who truly loves grows familiar with solitude. All human relationships, particularly those of love, leave us standing alone in a way that points toward the one relationship for which we hunger and toward which we move. Love, intimate human love—its presence as well as its absence—awakens and reawakens the sense that we are participating in a mystery far beyond our comprehension and that God continues to beckon us in the most human of ways.

Sister Anna Polcino, S.C.M.M., M.D., founder and international psychiatric director of the House of Affirmation, International Therapeutic Center for Clergy and Religious, is a member of the Medical Mission Sisters. Dr. Polcino received her degree from the Medical College of Pennsylvania. Following a surgical residency at Hahnemann Hospital, Philadelphia, she worked for nine years as a missionary surgeon and medical director at Holy Family Hospital in Pakistan and Bangladesh. Dr. Polcino then returned to the United States, completed a psychiatric residency at Worcester State Hospital, and pursued further postgraduate medical studies at Harvard University. A member of the American Psychiatric Association, the American Medical Association, the Massachusetts Medical Society, and the National Federation of Catholic Physicians, she is current editor of the *Bulletin* of the National Guild of Catholic Psychiatrists. Dr. Polcino is consultant and lecturer to clergy and religious in the United States and abroad.

Wholeness in Relationship to God

Anna Polcino

Of all our relationships, the most important one is with God. We build this relationship on the foundation of our existential loneliness, with the help of the virtues of faith, hope, and love. Fr. Raphael Simon, a psychiatrist and a Trappist monk, has said that to fall in love with God is the greatest of all romances, to seek him is the greatest of all adventures, and to find him is the greatest human achievement. I hope that when you have read and reflected on this chapter, you will agree with him. After all, we are here on earth to develop a union with the triune God, and through that, to be for others.

So let us begin by looking at loneliness, an inevitable part of being human. Each of us is a solitary individual, a person uniquely alone in this world. We can use our loneliness creatively, and thus grow more sensitive to the true and beautiful in life. Pain and isolation can lead us to a new knowledge of self. When we confront loneliness, we realize that our desires and yearnings far surpass our human limitations, and so in the end we can be satisfied only by God. Loneliness is an opportunity for each of us to achieve a closer intimacy with the living God.

How shall we define loneliness? It is not isolation; it is not being alone. We can be lonely in the midst of a group of people: with our families at home, with fellow professionals at work. Sometimes the presence of friendly people makes us realize how lonely we are. At the same time, some men and women can exist

29

in isolation for long periods of time without experiencing loneliness.

What then is loneliness? It is a prolonged state of mental pain or anguish caused by a sense of separation. It is a feeling of being a nonentity, of nonbeing, of nothingness, experienced in the depths of our being. Paul Tillich called it "the pain of being alone." When we are lonely we are aware that we are separated from others, sometimes from the very source of community. No one cares for us. This feeling of loneliness cannot be reduced to a single emotion. The cause of our loneliness may be separation from or loss of a loved one, a lack of communication, rejection, or deception. So we may feel longing or emptiness or frustration or bitterness. Whatever the feeling, we are distinctly aware of being alone as we go through each day, moving through a world of other people who may also be lonely.

I am sure, talking to your experience as a reflective person, that you have at times felt like a nonentity. No matter how many close friends you may have, still you sometimes experience a hunger and a terrible deep loneliness.

To ignore loneliness only intensifies its effects. People try to escape from loneliness in a number of ways that vary in effectiveness and positive qualities. They may join the crowd, go where people are. They may spend hours watching television, absorbed in the make-believe world of happy endings. They may use drugs or alcohol to obliterate the present. They may throw themselves into their work as an excuse to say they have no time for relationships. They may read books on how to be popular and try to be more outgoing. They may choose to be independent of others, to assert themselves as they are.

I believe there are three positive ways to deal with loneliness. First, we must learn to be alone with ourselves. We have to become aware of this existential feeling, to own it. We must spend time with it, willing to be alone, and not seek others to assuage our loneliness. Then we must learn to be with and for others. Finally, we must realize that this existential experience of loneliness can lead us to a closer union with God.

Being Alone

The first step toward conquering loneliness is to get in touch with ourselves, to be. We need to face the bright and dark sides of our natures and to accept them. We need to be strong, to let the feelings and expressions of our own identities flow. Never mind that others want to change us and mold us. We have a responsibility and a right to be true to ourselves.

When we need to express an emotion that we know the world does not wish to hear or will fail to affirm, we will feel tension. Still we must express ourselves, even though we do not please others and life is made more difficult.

Staying in touch with our own selves is an essential part of winning this battle to be. First we must work to be comfortable with ourselves, then analyze what other people tell us about ourselves. Before God, deep in our hearts, we can reflect on their opinions and decide if we should own these things. Often we experience this struggle alone, feeling imposed upon yet determined to triumph. In this time of solitude, we can learn to know ourselves better, make our choices, and end our confusion and depression.

While we struggle in this lonely silence to restore our spirit, we need strong, completely affirming voices. We need people who can appreciate this experience of loneliness, and not do us a disservice by trying to draw us away from it. They need to encourage us to stay with the experience, risking the darkness.

Sometimes in reviewing our past experiences, we find that the absence of love has stunted our growth, that we have been unable to express or even to admit our love for others. When we realize this lack of growth in our lives, we need someone to help us see our good qualities, someone who can appreciate the person we are and the person we can become. In this way we can move from loneliness to the solitude of soul that promotes inner growth.

Another important aspect of loneliness is the physical side. We are made up of body and soul, each affecting the other. We must be careful that loneliness does not result from neglecting our bodies. We cannot give of ourselves twenty-four hours a day, seven days a week. We must replenish ourselves. We can develop a sense of leisure and make time for it, cultivate interests outside our work. We should take time for vacations separate from the days we take for retreat or recollection, without feeling guilty. If we do not take care of our bodies, they will break down. We will be discouraged easily; problems will loom larger than they really are, and we will be unable to use as a grace the loneliness we experience.

By accepting loneliness we can more easily arrive at the center of our being where God in Trinity resides. Communion with God will grow and sustain us when we are separated from family and friends. Although our work may help to dispel loneliness, we need a deep personal prayer life to prevent our being distressed when alone. Through this inner life, we will be able to accept anguish and aridity in a peaceful way. Sometimes God permits us to experience loneliness in order to draw us nearer to him, or to make us more compassionate. However, even if we take care of our physical needs and reach out to others in friendship, we must still come to grips with loneliness. At such times we have only God.

Loneliness to Solitude

Solitude is not necessarily physical isolation, but a state of being alone, of inwardly directed consciousness. In solitude we claim value for ourselves as free beings. Turning inward enables us to discover the value of self-determination and responsibility. In solitude we examine our lives and praise or blame ourselves; we judge our successes and failures by our own standards. We find self-worth in solitude, in the core of our freedom. In simpler words, solitude is being alone and being happy about it, not feeling we always have to be with another. I think once you begin to develop the need for solitude, you grow to appreciate this private time and guard it jealously.

A seeking of healthy solitude is a recurring theme in the Scriptures. John the Baptist went into the desert; Christ went away from the crowd to pray. I often think of the time Christ left the multitude on the land and got into a boat, going apart to pray. I do not think he felt guilty about taking that time: he knew he deserved it. Do we think the same way?

The better we know ourselves, the better we will understand others. Solitude is necessary for our spiritual and professional growth. We need time to ponder about the persons to whom we minister. We need time to reflect on the skills that are necessary in our ministry. Solitude gives us the ability to face ourselves, others, and God.

The goal of solitude is love: love and acceptance of ourselves as we are and where we are, and love and compassion for others. Solitude must be based on prayer, meditation, and finally, contemplation. Just as we experienced a sexual awakening that led to maturity, so we must experience a spiritual awakening. The experience of intense spiritual desire, a desire for communion with God, can occur at any time, though we may not recognize it as such. But this desire for communion is a religious identity process that moves us to respond.

Another important aspect of becoming a spiritual person is decision or commitment. When we experience a spiritual awakening we become aware of our inner spiritual dimensions. We accept who we are. We realize we are called by God to a new life, a particular vocation, or a special time of renewal or conversion on a deeper level within our present vocation. This commitment involves responsibility: I do not concentrate solely on myself. I am responsible to others and to society.

Loneliness helps us grow in faith. We listen to God and discover our potential—for living, for serving others. Loneliness can be our road to spiritual maturity.

Value of Faith

As human beings, we need to be open to the progress of the future; faith can fulfill this need. The God of the Bible is the God of the Promise and the Covenant, and the religion of the Bible is a religion centered on the future. Faith assures us that we are loved and that our only duty is to accept being loved throughout life.

The most difficult task I face as a therapist is to convince men and women that they are lovable. They are so resistant to this idea that therapy can take months or years. These persons are not always to blame: they have learned through deprivation or rejection to see themselves as unworthy of love. If we really believe that God loves us with our own uniqueness, not as part of the mass of humanity, we will be amazed at what we can accomplish in our lives. In other words, take God literally. I have done so many times and never been disappointed.

Another value of faith centers on our search for self-fulfillment. By going out to others, by forgetting and transcending ourselves, we can experience true fulfillment. We will receive from others only in the measure that we give ourselves—not some *thing* but ourselves. By faith we dedicate ourselves to the Other and to all others. So faith, well understood and well lived, fulfills us by freeing us from our selfishness.

Next we need to develop in ourselves an active readiness to be open to everything that comes from God, not only during prayer but throughout the day. Listening should be our constant attitude. There is a constant interaction between listening in prayer and listening to everyday events. Listening in one area makes possible and promotes listening in the other.

If we learn to listen, just to be present, to be quiet and try to hear what God is telling us, we will develop an habitual awareness. Such an attitude will have neurophysiological components also, because we are not listening as separate spiritual entities. As we learn to listen for God's direction, we learn at the same time to listen to the people we encounter daily, for they all speak to us of God. Living in this holistic way, we will appreciate even more the virtues of faith, hope, and love.

Faith

Today we hear so much about the crisis of authority, the crisis of celibacy, the crisis in the Church. In reality it sounds like a new crisis every week. I think of a crisis as an opportunity. It is also a danger, but more important, it is an opportunity to evaluate. As one Dominican priest put it, "All this fuss over celibacy is really a crisis of the mind, and not of the flesh." It is true. At the basis of difficulties with authority, the discussions on celibacy, the changing role of religious orders in today's Church, is a question of faith. The reason for celibacy is *belief* in its value as a witness to service and union with Christ. Authority and celibacy can have meaning only when considered in the light of faith.

Faith is the foundation for all our actions and reactions within the Church. It is important, therefore, to ask ourselves what use we make of this faith of ours. We were taught that the act of faith is an act of the intellect, an act of the mind. Certainly it is, but it is also much more. The Bible does not mean intellectual assent when it speaks of faith. Abraham, our father in faith, did not merely assent to the truth of one God. He left everything to follow the will of that one God. He followed with his whole being, with his whole person.

Faith is an engagement of the whole person, not just of the intellect. *I* make the act of faith, not my intellect, not my ego, not my brain, not my will—I as a person. In English a synonym for faith is belief, belief meaning love. To believe means really to be love, to love completely, to give oneself without reserve.

The Latin of the Creed uses rather unusual grammar. A Latinist would say, "Credo Deo," not "Credo in Deum." But I believe there is a profound meaning to this expression. We translate it into English as "I believe in God." Literally we are saying, "I believe into God"—I believe into the Father, into the Son, into the Holy Spirit.

Faith, therefore, is much more than an act of the intellect assenting to the truth of three persons in one God. As Saint Thomas said a long time ago: "Faith relates not to the statement of dogma, but to the reality which it expresses." For us, then, faith is entering into a relationship with the Creator, the Redeemer, the Sanctifier. It is an encounter, a commitment of self to Another. That is why I think Saint Thomas, at the end of his life, having used his intelligence to try to understand God, finally reached that point where his whole being had entered into a contemplative gaze. He could no longer talk about who or what God is. He was speechless. That contemplative state is where we should arrive someday. A theologian whose studies do not influence or infiltrate his or her whole being would do better never to have studied theology. I would say the same for any subject, no matter how mundane or "profane." If it does not have some effect on you as a person, bring you somehow closer to God, it would be as well not to study. If my medical knowledge does not help me to become a better person so that I can relate to God, believe in him on a deeper level, commit myself to him, then what does it avail me? I am just a technician. Knowledge in any area can make this kind of holistic contribution.

If we look at marriage, we can get another idea of faith. The word fidelity occurs several times in the marriage rite. "Accept this ring as a pledge of my fidelity, as my promise that I will keep the faith." What a personal commitment the word faith is here. The young man who makes this act of faith hands himself over to his bride and unborn children, all of himself, heart, mind, skills, strength, bodily affections. Do not tell him faith involves only the intellect. He knows all it involves.

I can speak this way because of the experience of my nephew, who came to Massachusetts several years ago to study, met a young woman, and married her. I watched that relationship grow, the faithfulness the two young people exchanged, and the way they dialogued. The three of us often talked about religion and other serious matters, and I saw what fidelity meant to two people. So on the deepest level, faith is really an I-Thou relationship, not an I-It one. Faith commits you to someone. What do you make of this one, this someone; what do you make of God; what do you make of Christ? Periodically you should think about these questions. What does Christ mean to you? What does God, what does the Holy Spirit mean to you? Do you really believe the Holy Spirit dwells in your very depths?

In *Listening with the Third Ear* Theodore Reich talks about how the unconscious of the therapist speaks to the unconscious of the client. When I read his theory I thought, "But I believe it is deeper than that. I think it is the Holy Spirit in me, trying to tell me how I should guide this person." And the Holy Spirit in the unconscious of that man or woman is telling that person to be open: "Let yourself become vulnerable; trust in this therapist." So I think in the psychotherapeutic relationship many times it is not just the unconscious, purely technical type of communication that takes place, but the Holy Spirit. Many times in therapy one does not know what to say or do. One really does not. At those moments, I pray, "Holy Spirit, I don't know what to do." And I become quiet. Then, before I know it, just my presence is sufficient to bring that person through, to give some insight, or just to let that person be if he or she is angry. It is good to let people express anger. Sometimes clients get very angry, and I feel like cringing and think, "What have I done?" Actually, I know I have not done anything. I am there just to absorb their awakening emotions.

Having this faith does not mean we will be free of doubts. I believe doubts will come naturally about God, about life, about our own role in life, its meaning for us. Answers may not come so easily. It is not up to faith to supply the answers. Faith deals with the unseen and rests in mystery. These reflections and doubts can form the backdrop for a true act of faith, a deliberate renewal of our commitment despite our misgivings. Tillich spoke of this faith as being characterized by courage—not the soldier's courage, but the courage of the person who feels all the riddles of life and yet can say yes to life. There is a connection between faith and fortitude, between our commitment and our living it out. The Church will always need prophets to remind us that the grace of faith is one that costs. When prophets introduce areas of concern and doubt, they give faith a new and deeper meaning. Some prophets are exiled from their community as Teilhard de Chardin was: people who are not prominent, who have not written books, yet who may be prophets and may have to leave a particular community. However, many prophets choose to remain as Chardin did.

Since Vatican II the Church has struggled to be and needs every prophet the Holy Spirit can send us. But perhaps even more than prophets, the Church needs martyrs, men and women who will witness not only by their blood, but in many cases by remaining faithful to the Church as she is, while they are also faithful to their inner vision of what the Church should be.

In this kind of fortitude lies one source of the greatness of a man like Chardin. He knew the many frailties of the Church and suffered from the mistakes and timidity of those in authority. But the more obedience seemed to frustrate his deepest longings, the more firmly he declared his faith in the Jesuits and in the Church. He saw himself as needing to be ever more a Jesuit. He believed that if Christ really wished Chardin to proclaim him, it should be from a place in the ranks of the faithful.

There is another reason that faith requires fortitude. Our faith is indeed private and deeply personal; it is the I-Thou between each individual and God. But paradoxically, at the same time it has also a social or corporate nature. In baptism we receive faith by being incorporated into a community, and we continue to have faith in this way. God gives us his life, not directly but indirectly, not privately but corporately. What does this mean? It means we do not have faith either by ourselves or for ourselves. Faith is not private but social. Faith in people is sustained by actual grace. We ourselves are the world's preeminent actual grace.

Marshall McLuhan said that the medium is the message. It is not so much the what of the message as the how. To a certain extent this is true of all of us. What are people looking for when we stand before them? Not for what we say. They are looking for us. We are the message. In their need, they look to us as unfailing towers of strength, not realizing or understanding that like the apostles, we too can be of little faith. Whether we like it or not, we with our weaknesses, mean, selfish, and unfaithful as we are, are signs of faith for others, confirming or destroying that faith, confirming also that we are human. It is at such times that we need others to support us when our own human weakness comes through. They are the actual graces for us as we are for others.

What is actual grace? Well, we could give some kind of theological answer, but for me it is always *you*. We talk about the dark night of the soul, and people think we have to have some kind of mystical experience or some great revelation. There is a whole trend now of going to the desert. People do not realize the desert is within us. In the midst of a busy city we can experience the desert, and the dark night of the soul is going to be just the natural raw material of everyday relationships, everyday situations that God will use to purify us, to bring us close to him.

Hope

In addition to faith, we need hope and love. I am not going to discuss love at length because I think you know much about it already. I merely want to tell you what our foundress, Mother Anna Dengel, once told us about love:

> If you have real love, you are inventive. If you love, you try to find out, you are interested. If you really love, you are patient and long-suffering. Certainly if you love you accommodate yourself. If you love, you want to give—you are tireless, selfless, and generous. If you love, you really want to serve and not just work. One does not spare oneself if one loves.

I think that is a very beautiful description of love that contains much of what I have already said. Now I wish to say a little about hope and what faith teaches us.

A distinctive feature of Christianity is its proclamation of the resurrection, of hope. Some have interpreted this message to mean the establishment of a religion of salvation in the sense of release from this world. However, Dietrich Bonhoffer called this attitude a dangerous mistake. He believed that deliverance from cares and needs, from fears and longings, from sin and death into a better world beyond the grave is not the true picture of Christianity as it was proclaimed in the gospels and by Paul.

Bonhoffer suggested that Christianity offers a view of ordinary life in its ordinariness and that Christian hope sends us back to our life on earth. Critics have found many ambiguities in Bonhoffer's thought, but some of his insights are truly prophetic and profound. The Little Flower, Saint Therese, also spoke of Christianity as being the ordinary things of life.

Bonhoffer's insight into this notion of the ordinariness of Christianity could inspire us to call him, like Chardin, an apostle of hope, an apostle of affirmation: affirmation of the world in which we live, the world in which we work, pray, and love, the world in which we are to become holy—affirmation of ourselves as we are in this world. For too long spiritual writers have emphasized the opposition between the world and the spirit, inspired by Christ's words, "I have taken you out of the world." Too often this attitude became a call to retreat from the world. The emphasis was on withdrawal from the world as a necessary condition for holiness. Thus, contemplatives were considered the holiest men and women; they only used "worldly" things (baking bread, making cheese) to achieve that state. The attitude was that in order to be holy one leaves the world. I believe in contemplative life and hold that there is a need for it, but that separatist attitude affected the apostolic religious orders as well. Their members needed to be with people but were kept isolated from them. Thank God, this attitude is changing now.

Charles Peguy criticized this attitude in a powerful way when he said,

> To mount to God is not to abandon the world. Because pious people haven't the strength to face nature, they think they have made spiritual progress. Because they have no temporal courage, they think they have entered into the eternal. Because they have not courage to play their part in the world, they think they are doing God's work. Because they have not the courage to commit themselves to a human cause, they think they are serving God's cause. Because they do not love anyone, they think they love God.

This indictment stresses our need to accept the world on its own conditions. Our appeal as pastoral ministers, as religious educators, or whatever our work, must be to men and women who live in this world and whose responses are conditioned by all sorts of pressures.

We have all experienced these pressures in our own personal lives. What have they shown us? I believe it is our weakness that we do those things, as Paul says, that we will not do, that we are incomprehensible even to ourselves. Who of us can explain to ourselves the reasons for everything we do? I cannot. I am sure you cannot. It is this incomprehensibility, this general condition of weakness, that we must learn to accept. We must come to see this frailty not as something outside of God's plan for us, but rather, as part of it.

The Way of Weakness

Someone has said that every essential form of spiritual life is marked by ambiguity. This observation is certainly true of the Christian who finds life in death, joy in suffering, and strength in weakness. It is also the way God chooses to come to us. Bonhoffer observed that God is weak and powerless in the world. He took our sicknesses and carried our diseases for us. Thus it is not by his omnipotence that Christ helps us but by his weakness and suffering. Christ chose the way of weakness as the way to be with us, because it is the human condition. In the suffering Christ we recognize a true man, and in that recognition, we realize that it is foolish to dream of ever being completely free from suffering, from our own weakness. I believe this acceptance is good, for our weaknesses, our fears, even our sins can be the very stuff out of which holiness is made. What is the raw material of the dark night of the soul but our sins and our failures? An important point to remember is that for some men and women, to regress means to grow. The person has to regress, to be sinful, in order to learn what it means to become whole and to grow. Not that I am advocating sin!

In this way all things work together for the good of those who love God, as Paul tells us. Saint Augustine boldly adds, "all things, even sins." I love Saint Augustine's expression, "Love God and do what you will." There is a wealth of material in that saying because you can love God and take risks and live life fully, to the hilt. I believe that is what he really means.

There is a dynamism even in weakness. C. S. Lewis expressed this idea rather beautifully when he indicated that salvation might not consist in cancelling moments of sin but in the perfected humility (or I would say honesty) that bears the shame forever, rejoicing in furnishing an occasion for God's mercy and glad that the sin is common knowledge to others.

His observation reminds me of a seventy-year-old sister I had in therapy. I knew of her outside clinical practice as well loved, kind, and a beautiful presence. She came to see me one day to have a thorough physical examination, although she was in quite good health. However, she came to me primarily because she wanted to tell me something she had never revealed to anyone else. This secret had kept her honest and nonjudgmental and understanding of others. She told me that periodically throughout her life she had been plagued with the habit of masturbation. I thought, "Here is a saint." She was very humble, because this problem that she had not been able to eradicate made her so nonjudgmental, so compassionate toward others. She did not relish the sin, but she accepted this limitation that she could not help.

I have never forgotten that sister. She taught me a great lesson, never to be *judgmental.* We never know what persons are struggling with down in their depths. In reality, your greatest vice can be your greatest virtue, and your greatest virtue can be your greatest vice. Take men and women who are so generous that their generosity gets them into trouble. They overwork. Think about that. What is your greatest virtue? It can also be your greatest vice. If you have the capacity to be a great sinner, you should relish it, because you also have the capacity to be the greatest saint. Some saints in their writings clamor what great sinners they are, and I often ponder that. Saint Augustine in his early years was very promiscuous; but there are other saints who did not commit any great sins in their lives. Yet they knew what they could become, that they were free. You too are free to choose to be a sinner. Such is the awesomeness in life, I think, but the glory, too, that you can choose to be a great saint.

So we have to learn to use our weaknesses as Christ did by accepting them freely as God's will for us. Our affirmation must be after the manner of Christ. Christ did not redeem us by dying, but by accepting his suffering and death. Did you ever think about that? Christ was going to die anyway, because he was human. He redeemed us because he accepted the death of crucifixion. It was a human act of freedom.

Now if we Christians are to become Christlike, then the same act of loving free choice must be at the very center of our whole consciousness. We want to choose to love everything that we do and everything that we are—but we are weak. Accept this frailty as God's way of making saints of us. Accept it as a way of identifying with Christ the victim. Accept it as God's way of reminding us of our dependence on and need of him. Affirming our weaknesses, we can offer them to God as the only things we can truly call our own. We can offer them to God as an area where he can show his mercy. I often reflect that I am grateful God is going to judge me, not human beings, because I can depend on God's mercy. He will be just, yet he will always temper his justice with mercy.

So offer these weaknesses as our share in the weakness and the passion of Christ. Paul could glory in his weaknesses, and in spite of them he could trust in God. "He who trusts in the Lord finds nothing but mercy all around him."

The result of this affirmation and this offering is an undisturbed peace, no longer a neurotic search for means of sanctity. Rather, we use the raw materials at hand to become holy, to see them and ourselves as God sees them and us, to offer all to him and to be patient with the whole world, but most of all with ourselves. You may remember the last entry in the diary of George Bernanos's country priest.

> It's all over now. The strange mistrust I had of myself, of my own being, has flown, I believe, forever. That conflict is done. I am reconciled to myself, to the poor, poor shell of me. How easy it is to hate oneself. True grace is in forgetting, yet if pride could die in us, the supreme grace would be to love oneself in all simplicity as one would love any member of the body of Christ. Does it really matter? Grace is everywhere.

Saint Therese, the Little Flower, observed that everything is a grace. If you really believe in that spiritual philosophy of life, no matter what happens, both joys and sorrows will have meaning for you. You will find God speaking to you.

So to be a Christian consists of believing and hoping that under God's providence we will succeed by failure. Our relationship with God, Christ, the Holy Spirit becomes whole when we spend the time alone with them in solitude. Then when we are with others, we can be for and with them freely, which in turn will add to wholeness in our relationship with God.

Neil Ryan Castronovo, Ph.D., a full-time psychotherapist at the House of Affirmation in Whitinsville, Massachusetts, received his doctorate in clinical psychology at Virginia Commonwealth University in Richmond, and completed his internship at Worcester State Hospital. He has taught at the high school and college levels, worked in clinical and supervisory capacities in clinical pastoral education, and served as educator and psychological consultant to the adult education program in the diocese of Richmond. He is a member of the American Psychological Association and the Massachusetts Psychological Association.

The Realm of Relationship:
When Words Are Not Enough

The topic of this chapter is the realm of relationship and underlying dimensions in relationships. Before looking at these underlying dimensions, however, I want to examine some of the parameters of "the realm of relationship" by juxtaposing a monologue from a contemporary film with a cursory overview of the relationship between God and his people as developed in the Old Testament. In this way I hope to provide a meaningful context for the application of psychological theory to relationships.

The Realm of Relationship

In the 1977 film *Annie Hall,* Woody Allen gives his own reflections on relationships after his main character has spent some time with his former lover, Annie Hall:

> After that it got pretty late and we both had to go. But it was great seeing Annie again. I realized what a terrific person she was and how much fun it was just knowing her. And I thought of that old joke, you know, that this guy goes to a psychiatrist and he says, "Doc, my brother's crazy, he thinks he's a chicken." And, ah, the doctor says, "Well, why don't you turn him in?" And the guy says, "I would but I need the eggs." Well, I guess that's pretty much how I feel about relationships. You know, they're totally irrational and crazy and

47

absurd and . . . but, I guess we keep going through it because,
ah, most of us need the eggs.[1]

I am convinced that each of us could reflect on relationships
in our lives, whether they be in the context of our family of
origin, friendships, romance, community, marriage, ministry,
or our spirituality, and get a flavor of what Woody Allen expresses here: relationships are replete with paradox, so hard to
understand, and so necessary to our lives. We all need the eggs.
Whereas this monologue captures the particular reflections on
relationships of a middle-aged Jewish actor/writer in 1977, just
a quick overview of the relationship between God and his chosen
people as recorded in Scripture adds more of a universal touch
to the same theme.

The abrupt nature of God's call of Abraham and his people to
a lasting relationship leaves them and us in awe and wonder concerning the motivation and source of relationship: Why them?
Why me? Why now? In the Exodus account we experience the
vast fluctuations of thoughts, hopes, feelings, and dreams that
constitute the realm of relationship.

The Jewish community fluctuates from the triumphant song
of victory (Exod. 15) and their pledge, "All that Yahweh has
said, we will do" (Exod. 19:8) to their return to their apostasy in
the form of worshiping other gods (Exod. 32) and their doubts
in the desert: "Why did we not die at Yahweh's hand in the land
of Egypt? You have brought us to this wilderness to starve this
whole company to death!" (Exod. 16:3).[2]

It is not the Jewish people alone who express their need for
"the eggs" in this relationship, but God also. His words, spoken
through the prophets, are not those of a disinterested, dispas-
sionate deity, but of a God who expresses disappointment,
anger, and jealousy: "Israel knows nothing, my people understand nothing" (Isa. 1:3); "I will not love her children, since

---

1. Diane Jacobs, *But We Need the Eggs: The Magic of Woody Allen*
(New York: St. Martin's Press, 1982).

2. Scripture quotes are taken from The Jerusalem Bible (New York:
Doubleday, 1966).

they are children of whoring. . . . It is Yahweh who is speaking. That is why I am going to block her way with thorns" (Hos. 2:6, 8). The paradoxical words of this jealous God in relationship with his people continue: "I will betroth you to myself forever, betroth you with integrity and justice, with tenderness and love; I will betroth you to myself with faithfulness, and you will come to know Yahweh" (Hos. 2:21-22).

What Woody Allen refers to as the "totally irrational and crazy and absurd" quality of relationships is further explicated in the relationship between God and Job in one of the Wisdom Books as Job, "a sound and honest man who feared God and shunned evil" (Job 1:1), wrestles with the age-old question: can an all-good and all-powerful God allow evil to befall those in relationship to him? "I stand before you, but you take no notice. You have grown cruel in your dealings with me, your hand lies on me, heavy and hostile" (Job 30:21). And so the questions and struggles rage down through the history of mutual relationship between God and human beings and between one person and another.

I have elaborated on the parameters of the realm of relationship to illustrate the centrality of relationship to the experience of being persons—human and divine. The need for right relationships cuts across personalities, cultures, and religions. When we talk about relationships, we are at the bedrock. In the beginning is the relationship—as "God's spirit hovered over the water" (Gen. 1:2), and as John tells us, "In the beginning was the Word" (John 1:1). Indeed, it seems that needing the eggs, the need to be in relationship, is constitutive of personhood.

Psychology and Relationship

Given this wide context of the realm of relationship, can psychological theory provide us with any helpful understanding of relationships? I would say a qualified yes: qualified in the sense that we cannot demand simple answers to very profound questions. I view the practice of psychology as an art based on an emerging science. As a practicing psychologist, I must use both my creativity and my disciplined training to help bring some order out of chaos. There is no prior guarantee that this process will succeed. If order does come out of chaos, it is through a mutual process in the context of relationship. Therefore, both in this discussion and in the therapeutic relationship, the success of psychology in bringing meaningful understanding and change depends upon reciprocal interaction. The insights that I present here will necessarily be limited or facilitated by the reciprocal interaction between reader and author.

A major psychological contribution to our understanding of relationship was provided by the insights and clinical work of an American psychiatrist, Harry Stack Sullivan. Sullivan's interpersonal theory of psychiatry differed markedly from Sigmund Freud's emphasis on intrapsychic phenomena. Sullivan viewed personality as "the relatively enduring pattern of recurrent interpersonal situations which characterize a human life."[3] He believed that since the individual does not and cannot exist apart from his or her relations with other people, the proper study of psychiatry and psychology is the interpersonal field. From the first day of life we are part of an interpersonal situation, and throughout the rest of our lives we remain members of a social field. Even the man who resigns from society and becomes a hermit carries with him into the wilderness memories of former personal relationships which continue to influence his thinking and acting. Sullivan believed "we are all much more closely human than otherwise,"[4] and that, at least to a minor extent, at times we all deal with another person as if he or she were someone else, usually a close person from our past interpersonal lives. When these interpersonal distortions cause appreciable difficulties in our daily living, they are clearly unhealthy and may require professional treatment. It is important to note, however, that Sullivan believed we all are subject to these distortions, and that our

---

3. H. S. Sullivan, *The Interpersonal Theory of Psychiatry* (New York: Norton, 1953), p. 111.

4. H. S. Sullivan, *Conceptions of Modern Psychiatry* (Washington, D.C.: The William Alanson White Psychiatric Foundation, 1947), p. 7.

relationships can be enhanced by our growing awareness of them and ability to respond flexibly in interpersonal situations.

Because of his emphasis on the interpersonal, Sullivan placed great importance on communication. Much research and many clinical applications have been derived from a focus on communications as defining the realm of relationship. From a communications perspective we can define and measure any relationship as the present and cumulative result of reciprocal communication messages between persons, messages that are both verbal and nonverbal.[5] In human communication there are always two levels of messages, both sent and received. The first level is the more obvious content level, expressed by words. But there is always a simultaneous relationship level to all communication, which occurs along nonverbal channels; it is this second level of communication, which is mostly nonintentional and automatic, that primarily defines relationship. It is on the second level of communication that two persons in relationship make mutual claims on how they want to be perceived and reacted to—in a sense pulling from each other validation of each person's self-image. Again in primarily nonverbal ways we mutually respond to this "pull" through emotional, cognitive, and imaginal responses, which further define the ongoing communication.

I am going to illustrate these two levels of communication and how they define relationship by pretending that you are present here with me. Right now on the first level of communication I am using words to communicate with you, and you are interpreting what I am saying in terms of the universal symbolic meanings contained in the words I am using. This is the first and simplest level of communication. But simultaneously I am sending many nonverbal messages to you, mostly unintentionally and automatically, which have already begun to define our relationship (through my eye contact, facial expressions, head and

5. Some ideas in this section are taken from Donald J. Kiesler, "A Communication Analysis in Psychotherapy," *Psychiatry* 42 (1979): 299-311.

body movements, and gestures as well as my paralanguage—
tone, pitch, voice variation). Although you may have been mostly silent on the verbal channel of communication, nevertheless
you also are sending nonverbal messages defining your relationship to me (your eye contact, stillness or restlessness, head nods,
smiles, yawns). Implicit in my nonverbal behavior is my claim as
to how I want to be perceived and reacted to by you. Part of the
claim of which I am aware is that I want you to see me as
respectful, empathic, competent, and challenging. Already I
have stimulated in you through my words but primarily through
my nonverbal behavior certain positive and negative reactions,
behavioral tendencies, and cognitions—all of which are taking
place inside you (although because of their unintended and
automatic functioning you may not have been aware of them until now). Whether or not we are aware of them, our mutual
nonverbal behaviors and simultaneous responses are defining
right now the relationship level of our communication. Whether
or not we use words, we cannot *not* communicate. We are constantly in relationship, primarily through this nonverbal level of
interaction.

In referring back to Woody Allen's reflections on relationships as "totally irrational and crazy and absurd," we can respond that the realm of relationship has a logic and communication channel of its own, very different from the denotative, verbal level each of us spends so much time focusing upon, acquir-
ing, and perfecting. In the realm of relationship words are not
enough; frequently they get in the way; and sometimes they actually contradict the true relationship message. Think, for example, of the man who tenses his facial muscles and pounds his fist
on the table as he exclaims, "I love my wife!" Which message
comes through more clearly? Indeed, relationships are not absurd in the sense that they can never be given meaning. They are,
however, inherently ambiguous because meaning in relationships is always being negotiated primarily on this second level of
communication. Meaning is never fixed and must constantly be
won in relationships.

If we were to focus merely on the linguistic level of the relationship between God and his people as outlined above, we would be forced to conclude that this is a pretty crazy pattern of relationship—God's call and promise of eternal love, his people's promise of fidelity, their broken promises, punishment, repentance, conversion, and the cycle begins again and again. But what pervades the Scriptures and goes much deeper than the words is the mutual ongoing and primarily nonverbal renegotiation of meaning in relationship in the form of history, ritual, and the unbroken bond of covenantal love. The essence of relationships transcends the verbal, the logical, and the demand for fixed security.

Gaining Access to the Realm of Relationship

The thesis presented here, then, is that the crucial place to search for relationship is in nonverbal communication, which is the language of emotion and relationship. It is important to emphasize that when I speak of nonverbal communication I am not referring to a simplistic process of translating nonverbal behaviors into fixed categories and set meanings. To approach nonverbal behavior and the realm of relationship with the demands of the denotative, logical analysis common to the linguistic channel of communication is akin to translating poetry into prose—into words that have lost their vitality.

We approach the realm of relationship on its own terms. From the perspective presented in this chapter, it is clear that any meaningful reflection on relationship must take place in the context of ongoing relationships. Books and words can be helpful sources on the informational level of communication. However, when we enter the realm of relationship, this second level of communication, we need one another to make us conscious of the things we cannot see alone. In the remainder of this chapter, I shall look at three underlying dimensions in relationship and illustrate them through a specific interpersonal interaction.

Relationship in Interaction

> At daybreak he appeared in the temple again, and as all the people came to him, he sat down and began to teach them. The scribes and Pharisees brought a woman along who had been caught committing adultery; and making her stand there in full view of everybody, they said to Jesus, "Master, this woman was caught in the very act of committing adultery, and Moses has ordered us in the law to condemn women like this to death by stoning. What have you to say?" They asked him this as a test, looking for something to use against him. But Jesus bent down and started writing on the ground with his finger. As they persisted with their question, he looked up and said, "If there is one of you who has not sinned, let him be the first to throw a stone at her." Then he bent down and wrote on the ground again. When they heard this, they went away one by one, beginning with the eldest, until Jesus was left alone with the woman, who remained standing there. He looked up and said, "Woman, where are they? Has no one condemned you?" "No one, sir," she replied. "Neither do I condemn you," said Jesus. "Go away, and don't sin any more."
>
> (John 8:1-11)

Biblical scholars are quite in agreement that this passage is misplaced, being more in line with the Synoptic Gospels and probably originally part of the Gospel of Luke. For our purpose this account presents a vivid picture of the preeminence of nonverbal behavior in the realm of relationship. The Pharisees in this account are masters of the linguistic informational level of communication. Jesus refuses to respond to them on this level and shifts to the nonverbal level of communication—he becomes silent, scribbles, makes a rather blunt and obvious comment, and returns to scribbling. His focus on the level of relationship confounds the Pharisees and leads to their withdrawal, leaving Jesus in relationship with the woman. This interaction provides the context for my discussion of the underlying dimensions in relationships.

Dimensions in Relationships

For years studies in social psychology have identified three dimensions or continua that constitute the domain of relationships. Psychologists who specialize in communications point to these dimensions as three major relationship issues that persons who partake in any interpersonal interaction are continually negotiating, mainly through nonverbal channels: inclusion (degree of importance in one's life), power or status (dominance or submission), and affiliation (love or hate).[6] When interacting with each other, our nonverbal behavior is continually expressing messages to the other participant as to how close or intimate we want to be with him or her, how much in charge or control we want to be, and to what extent we want to include that person as a continuing significant other in our lives.

Inclusion

To gain a flavor of inclusion issues in our lives, try now to imagine the following scenario:

You sign up for a three-week summer course entitled "Faith and Sexuality." Your anticipation is that this will be a lecture course with a maximum enrollment of one hundred students. You arrive on the first day, notebook in hand, and you find that you and six other students will meet with the professor for seminar discussions and activities that will focus upon the members' reflection on and sharing of their own lived experiences of faith and sexuality. Placing yourself in such a situation, what are your initial thoughts, feelings, and behaviors? Your reactions are reflective of your own approach to inclusion issues.

The most basic dimension of relationships, both in terms of child developmental issues and of forming any new individual or group relationship, is inclusion, or the need to establish and maintain a satisfactory relation with others with respect to interaction and association. Inclusion expresses itself by behaviors that indicate the need to be in or out of dyads or groups. How

6. For a more complete theoretical consideration of these dimensions, see William C. Schutz, *The Interpersonal Underworld* (Palo Alto, Cal.: Science and Behavior Books, 1966).

involved can I be or am I willing to be with the other(s)? Can I trust my real self to the other? In order to be included, a person must have a definite identity so that he or she can be distinguished from others. Important components of inclusion are prominence, recognition, prestige, individuality, and interest.

When our interpersonal developmental history includes experiences of successful resolution of inclusion relations, on a deep level we feel worthwhile and significant. We can be comfortable both with people and alone, and can flexibly show either high or low participation in relationships without undue anxiety. Such men and women are capable of commitment and involvement but can also withhold them if they judge it appropriate.

Unsuccessful resolution in the area of inclusion results in anxieties that the self has no value, that it is worthless and empty and not important enough to receive attention. This attitude can lead to a basic fear of isolation and abandonment, perhaps the most potent of all interpersonal fears. People respond to such fears behaviorally in very different ways. Rather than risk being ignored by others, some choose to stay away from people and push themselves toward a stance of self-sufficiency. Behind this withdrawal, they may harbor feelings of hostility at not being understood. Another way of behaviorally responding to these anxieties concerning inclusion is to focus or force attention on oneself, always seeking companionship and not being able to tolerate being alone. There are many direct and subtle manifestations of both of these extreme behavioral modes of coping with anxieties concerning inclusion. However, their roots lie in the basic lack of feeling worthwhile enough to choose either to break into or to remain outside relationships in ways that are flexible, meaningful, and satisfying to self and to important others in one's interpersonal life.

In the passage from the Gospel of John cited above, Jesus' behaviors clearly and directly communicate his sense of identity, prominence, and his discretion concerning with whom he was willing to enter into relationship. He shows his comfort with his role as teacher, refusing the pull from the Pharisees to act as judge. Lack of eye contact and physical withdrawal from the Pharisees indicate Jesus' refusal to enter into relationship with them on their terms, an unwillingness to play games at the expense of this woman's predicament. With remarkable clarity and forcefulness he communicates a truth similar to Sullivan's insight that "we are all much more simply human than otherwise." Faced with a reflection on their own histories and identities, quite in contrast to Jesus' own comfort with who he is, the Pharisees withdraw, uncomfortable and anxious. We can only guess at their feelings. We know from their future actions that they harbor hostile feelings toward Jesus, perhaps stemming somewhat from their own unresolved inclusion needs.

Having dismissed the games of the Pharisees, Jesus can break into relationship with the woman standing before him. He does this with his presence, eye contact, and dialogue, behaviors that communicate interest and respect. We get the sense that he and this woman share a moment that communicates mutual satisfactory resolution of inclusion issues and feelings.

The dimension of inclusion involves the process of formation in relationships. As such, it requires resolution of some basic trust issues both initially and throughout the development of the relationship: How willing am I to trust my real self to another? What will this cost me? Do I feel worthwhile? Do I risk the pain of breaking into relationship without any guarantee? What makes this process difficult for each of us is that we have developed fundamental orientations toward interpersonal relations, patterns that bias our thoughts, feelings, and behaviors to expect in the present what we have experienced in the past. It takes renewed courage and work to challenge these biases and risk breaking into relationships in new ways.

Power

To gain a sense of the issues involved in the power dimension, try to imagine your responses to an interaction with the individual whose interpersonal style is described here:

Bobbie is a person who makes decisions like what to do or where to go when s/he is with others. Bobbie gives advice and information when others have decisions to make and often talks people into doing what s/he would like. S/he generally takes charge of things when with people and at the present time directs the activities of several clubs and associations to which s/he belongs. Bobbie generally seizes opportunities to instruct or explain things to others, which often leads her/him to dominate conversations, interrupting when others speak and "talking others down." Moreover, Bobbie orders friends and associates around and exploits or manipulates others for her/his own ends.[7]

Your imagined thoughts, feelings, and behaviors toward this individual whose interpersonal style is rigidly dominant can be helpful clues to the way you deal with interpersonal power issues.

Once relationships are formed, the dimension of power, status, or control is expressed along a continuum ranging from the desire for power, control, and authority over others and one's future to the desire to be controlled and have responsibility removed from oneself. Whereas being a prominent participant is important to one seeking inclusion, winning and being right, or at least being on the same side as the winner, is crucial to the control seeker. In relationships people take on or seek different status roles, and in this process key issues are power struggles, competition, and influence. Status expresses itself by feelings and behaviors of top-bottom: Who is in charge? Who makes the decisions in this relationship?

People who have successfully resolved status issues in their relations with others in childhood have a deep conviction that they are capable and responsible, neither shrinking from responsibility nor constantly striving to prove how competent they are. As the situation demands, they can feel comfortable in either giving or not giving orders and in either taking or not taking orders. They are not locked into rigid thought, feeling, and behavioral patterns in the area of control.

---

7. This description of the dominant interpersonal style was adapted from Donald J. Kiesler, *Manual for the Impact Message Inventory* (Richmond: Virginia Commonwealth University, 1979).

By contrast, those who have not successfully resolved conflicts in the status area are characterized by deep feelings of incompetence, irresponsibility, and the fear that others know their shortcomings. At one extreme are the submissive men and women who try to give up responsibility in interpersonal relationships by letting others make decisions, and who avoid situations in which they will feel helpless. They fear that they will be given more responsibility than they can handle and that others will not give help if they need it. Beneath their sense of incompetence are feelings of hostility and lack of trust toward others who might withhold assistance. At the other extreme are the dominant persons, fearful that if they are not at the top of the power hierarchy, they will be ruled and controlled by others.

Throughout the gospel account of Jesus' confrontations with the Pharisees, we repeatedly see references to two sources of power: *exousia,* authority or power that has been granted or socially licensed; and *dunamis,* a power unmediated by official social legitimation and experienced by others as raw power, spontaneous, uncontrollable, and often fearful. Although Jesus never denied the power of legitimately sanctioned authority, his own life and teachings are marked by an emphasis on *dunamis.* He exhibited this *dunamis* in relationship to others. This power went out from him to those who touched him (Mark 5:30). And as in the above account, Jesus encouraged persons to recognize and act upon their own *dunamis* in their relationship to God as well as to one another: no longer a dichotomy between God and humanity in terms of the opposition of "one up, the other down; one good, the other not-good; one with power, the other without; one giving, the other receiving; one in heaven, the other on earth, but rather a constellation of relation in which God is nothing other than the resource of relational *dunamis,* unable to be wholly contrasted or identified with any one person in any time or place."[8] Jesus began a relationship with this woman

---

8. Isabel Carter Hayward, *The Redemption of God: A Theology of Mutual Relation* (Washington, D.C.: University Press of America, 1982), p. 43.

with too much respect for her dignity as a person to act from a position of dominance. He entered into a dialogue with her, summoning her through the power of relation to get in touch with her own power in the immediacy of God being here now in relation.

Thus in our own lives it is only in relationship that we can negotiate the extremes of power. In the immediacy and power of relationships we inform the socially sanctioned authority given us by our education, vowed life, ordination, or office with the substance of human *dunamis*. True relationship exposes externally granted authority lacking in *dunamis* for what it is: fearfully empty, irresponsible, and incompetent. "When they heard this they went away, one by one, beginning with the eldest."

Each of us has experienced moments of anxiety in relationship when we have struggled with questions of our own authority, tempted to hide behind our socially licensed status. Fidelity to specific relationships calls us to risk renegotiation of power again and again as we grow in appreciation, flexibility, and comfort with a wide range of responses to power issues in relationship: Who is "calling the shots" here? How much can I push for what I want in this relationship? What is required of me? Can I say what I really think? Can I take it if others say what they really think? As in the other areas of relationship, nonverbal behaviors predominate in communicating our current resolution of the status dimension.

Affiliation

Affiliation behavior differs from inclusion and control in that it can occur only between two people at any one time. Both inclusion and control can either be dyadic or involve an interaction between one person and a group of people. Affiliation refers to an especially strong feeling between the two people involved, especially in the areas of love and hate in their various degrees. It is usually the last phase to develop in a human relation, and the central concern of affiliation is with the negotiation of how close or far a person is willing to move toward the other in relationship.

Persons who have successfully resolved affectional relationships with others in childhood can be comfortable in close emotional relationships as well as in situations requiring emotional distance. Such persons feel deeply that they are capable of being loved as well as of giving genuine affection. Although it is important for them to be liked, they can accept it if someone dislikes them without jumping to a generalized conclusion that they are unlovable persons.

The primary anxiety and deep conviction of men and women whose interpersonal behavior expresses an inadequate or an excessive need for affiliation is that the self is bad and nasty. Persons who express too little affiliation consciously try to keep their two-person relations on a superficial level, attempting to remain emotionally uninvolved for fear that if they were to try to satisfy their affectional needs, no one would love them. Avoidance of people, interpersonal antagonism, or being superficially friendly to everyone as a safeguard against getting close to any one person are all methods that these men and women may employ to maintain emotional distance. Persons who express excessive needs for affiliation may try to relieve their anxieties about being rejected and unlovable by always attempting to gain approval and being extremely personal, ingratiating, intimate, manipulative, or possessive. Both of these extreme interpersonal stances toward affiliation are accompanied by strong anxiety about being unlovable and contain considerable hostility stemming from the anticipation of rejection.

Although increasing physical distance marks the relationship between Jesus and the Pharisees in the above passage, Jesus and the woman share a momentary closeness. The primary nonverbal expression of affiliation is one of embrace (either literal or symbolic), the expression of deeper feelings. Whereas physical embrace is characteristic of many of Jesus' interpersonal interactions, in this meeting Jesus' symbolic gestures of presence, eye contact, personal respect, compassion, and admonition communicate his deeper feelings toward this woman, while his withdrawal and indifference to the games of the

Pharisees congruently communicate his disdain and distance from them.

In an age where the signs of the times are calling us to a renewed awareness of the centrality of relationships to the task of being more fully alive and human, we may find ourselves lost and confused. Our North American culture has prided itself on the attainments achieved through rugged individualism and the self-sufficiency of the nuclear family. Until recently, our Catholic tradition has chosen to emphasize interpersonal distance in its liturgical celebrations, in its excessive concern with sexual transgressions in the moral sphere, and in its harsh admonitions to celibate religious and priests to avoid particular friendships and to view heterosexual interactions as possible occasions of sin.

The challenge to renegotiate the issues of emotional and physical distance in relationships is one that causes confusion to both secular society and the Church, to celibates and noncelibates. Our common gospel call to be lovers of God and neighbor by establishing right and just relationships can be blocked by overly restrictive taboos on touch, closeness, presence: man to man, woman to woman, woman to man—between and among the married, single, and celibate states. Sullivan's theme that "we are all much more simply human than otherwise" again echoes in my mind as I reflect on how much we need one another to renegotiate again and again the issues of affiliation to help bring about right and just relationships, the essence of the kingdom of God: Am I willing to care and to show my care? What if no one cares for me? What if they do? Will I or others be able and willing to bear my expressed needs for affiliation?

Conclusion

Throughout this exploration of the underlying dimensions in relationships, I have emphasized the importance of flexibility in using a broad range of verbal and nonverbal behaviors to continually renegotiate interpersonal issues in the areas of inclusion, power, and affiliation. Indeed, from a communications perspective, abnormal behavior results from and builds on an individual's inability to detect and correct self-defeating, interpersonally unsuccessful aspects of communication, particularly as expressed in nonverbal behaviors.

By heightening our awareness of and responding to what I have described as the nonverbal language of emotion and relationships, we can affirm our need for relationship (we do need the eggs) without having to live with illusions and distortions about self and others. Approaching the realm of relationship on its own terms, we can begin to experience more satisfaction and fulfillment in our interpersonal interactions.

I have also stressed the central importance of relationships as the context for our growth as persons. The realm of relationship militates against the idolatry of fixed, unchanging, and safe interpersonal interactions. As we continue to risk entering this unsafe but good realm together in the community of faith, every once in a while we get glimpses of the reality that the time has indeed come and "the kingdom of God is close at hand" (Mark 1:15).

Reverend Thomas A. Kane, Ph.D., D.P.S., international executive director of the House of Affirmation, is a priest of the Roman Catholic diocese of Worcester. He pursued his undergraduate studies at St. Edward's University, Austin, Texas; his graduate studies at National University of Mexico, Rutgers University, and St. Bonaventure University; and his post-graduate studies at Boston University and the University of Birmingham, England. As an educator and psychotherapist, Fr. Kane is a consultant to several Roman Catholic and Protestant groups. He is a frequent lecturer to academic and medical communities in the United States and Europe and a visiting scholar at Harvard University. Fr. Kane is a member of several professional organizations, serves on the board of directors of the National Guild of Catholic Psychiatrists, and is the author of several publications.

The Celibate Renunciation

Thomas A. Kane

There is a story told of a Maine farmer who went to his small country church one Sunday. A visiting preacher from a divinity school in Boston was filling in for the regular minister. The preacher, noting that this lone farmer was the only person who had shown up for the service, remarked: "Surely you don't want me to preach to you alone in the church today?" "Don't know much about preachin'," said the farmer. "But I know a lot about cows, and I know if I had only one cow, I'd still have to feed her." The preacher got the point, ascended the pulpit, and preached for nearly an hour! At the end of the service he asked the farmer what he thought of the sermon. "Don't know much about preachin'," said the farmer. "But I know a lot about cows, and I know if I had only one cow to feed, I wouldn't feed her the whole darn load!"

Taking the farmer's wisdom to heart, I will not attempt to say everything there is to say about celibacy, but will offer only a few reflections that might challenge your thought and encourage your faith.

The Awkward

In the House of Affirmation symposium on happiness last year, I presented an essay on affirmation and relationships. I noted that as a result of their training, many priests and religious

65

are in a stage of development regarding their life of relationship that I call the *awkward* period.[1]

In that presentation I recalled the words of Karol Wojtyla, now John Paul II.

> It is exactly in this that the fundamental ethical trait of love is expressed: it is an affirmation of a person—without this affirmation, love does not exist. Permeated with a proper attitude concerning the value of a person— and such an attitude we termed affirmation—love reaches its fullness; it becomes what it ought to be: an integral love. Without this affirmation of the value of a person, love disintegrates and, in fact, does not exist at all, even if the reactions or experiences coming into play are of a "loving" (erotic) character.[2]

I then observed that healthy relationships enable celibates to live their unique life style. So important is this idea of relationship, I noted, that the United States Bishops Committee on Priestly Life and Ministry stated:

> Too often, stress which has been placed on avoiding relationships effects a defensive style when priests relate with women or when sisters relate with men, either socially or in ministry. Such style is particularly inappropriate today when men and women are expected to interact on a regular basis as co-workers as well as in social situations.

> Men and women must be able to interact in relationships which are mature, honest, responsible and appreciative. Such relationships presume a realistic degree of self-knowledge. Furthermore, they allow each person to realize his or her God-given dignity in the blend of femininity and masculinity within every person. This blend is God's gift to us and to each other. Men and women who are Church ministers, as much as any other human person, need one another's support in personal development. Celibate commitment must be a path toward the sort of independence, self-reliance and wholeness which make

---

1. The essay is fully developed in *Happiness: Issues of Emotional Living in an Age of Stress for Clergy and Religious,* ed. Thomas A. Kane (Whitinsville, Mass.: Affirmation Books, 1982), pp. 63-83.

2. Andrew N. Woznicki, *Karol Wojtyla's Existential Personalism* (New Britain, Conn.: Mariel Publications, 1980).

one capable of conscious self-sacrificing and loving relationships with others. Otherwise, it cannot be an appropriate lifestyle.[3]

I observed that this statement could be very dangerous. What is now being described as an appropriate way to maintain celibacy as a life style is not the way in which most present-day priests and religious were trained. Many were not educated in a manner that made their studies in scholastic philosophy an integrated approach to the intellectual and emotional life. A number of priests and religious have been exposed to a system that encouraged not a healthy discipline but fear of the emotional life.

Sigmund Freud was condemned in seminaries and by some schools of thought as a reductionist for supposedly claiming that all human relationships are sexual. Yet in regard to human relationships, seminarians, priests, and religious were taught to be on their guard not only with the opposite but with the same sex. What they heard explicitly condemned about Freud they were implicitly (some explicitly) taught about relations—all relationships will end in bed!

Professors condemned Freud's so-called reductionism but were often reductionists themselves regarding human relationships. The reality is that people go to bed because they choose to do so. Priests and religious, who are now being encouraged in relationships, who are now being told this is where the celibate witness is most real, are often confused and suspicious because of their previous training, and they enter relationships in a reductionist manner. By this I mean that they sometimes consciously or unconsciously are motivated by the belief that all behavior does indeed become genital at one time or another.

If we encourage priests and religious to enter relationships, as the documents of Vatican II* and the U. S. bishops' *As One Who*

3. U.S. Bishops Committee on Priestly Life and Ministry, *As One Who Serves* (Washington, D.C.: United States Catholic Conference, 1977), p. 65.

* Vatican II makes no distinction between the consecrated chastity of the religious and the celibacy of diocesan priests, at least in regard to motivation and practice.

Serves suggest, then we must not be frightened by some of the awkward growth we see in relationships. We need to be open to new models of relationships between men and women. For example, vacations for priests with fellow priests are usually deemed acceptable, and this is good; they are acceptable, too, if the vacation is with the priest's family, and this is frequently good; and sometimes even a vacation with a group of five or six parish altar boys is approved of, though why this is good is a mystery to me. But what would we say or not say to the priest who chooses to go on vacation with a woman friend? I am not necessarily advocating this behavior. I am suggesting that if we invite new insights and give new importance to male-female relationships, then we must be prepared for new models, new structures for relationships. Inviting mature male-female relationships will not only bring about a healthier understanding of celibacy but also invite us to reflect on its options.

Nonetheless, this stage of development many are now in, which I have chosen to call *awkward growth,* makes priests and religious ask tough questions about their sexuality. It is a period calling for a deep understanding of personal integrity and community responsibility.

Goals

The object of this essay is to look at the behavior of a particular kind of celibate, other than the awkward type I just mentioned. My purpose is not to consider optional celibacy itself nor to present a twelve-step lesson on how to be a celibate and enjoy it. Rather, what I intend to do is to invite you to look with me at the behavior of those celibates who view celibacy as a deeply meaningful and profoundly significant way to celebrate life.

The Proclaimers

In a thought-provoking essay entitled "The Psychology and Asceticism of Celibacy," Father Martin W. Pable, O.F.M. Cap., reminds us that celibacy by its very nature is an act of renunciation.[4] He points out that the Latin word *renuntiare* means "to proclaim again." It is an act of affirmation free of the negative connotations usually given to the word "renounce."

Such celibates, whom we can call the *proclaimers,* are not negating any human good or value; they are relativizing some values in order to give a more central place to others.

Before we respond to the query of just what these celibates are "proclaiming again," let us observe something of their behavior. First, these persons tell us that they have freely chosen celibacy.[5] For them celibacy is a way of loving others, as well as a freely chosen decision not to marry nor to engage in genital love.

Second, these celibates, these proclaimers, speak of their celibacy as rooted in a deep religious experience of the love of God: a religious experience based on deep Gospel values. They view their life style not so much as an opportunity to *give* but rather to *accept* the love of the Father in Jesus Christ. The fundamental religious experience is primarily one of receiving, not of giving.

Sidney Callahan notes that although celibacy may be very important to a Christian theology of sexuality, psychologically it is unexplored territory.[6] Noticeable in the psychological profile of the proclaimers is the fact that they usually come from families that are warm and affectionate without being smothering. These men and women have left family dependence behind and have formed new ties in a community of friends and fellow workers.

These celibates bear witness to and proclaim again some basic incarnational values, five of which are noted below.

1. *The value of sexuality*

Just as a sound does not exist unless it is perceived, the sexuality of a celibate cannot exist in a vacuum. Interaction with others is necessary. Thus, affirmation in the social sense requires

4. Martin W. Pable, "The Psychology and Asceticism of Celibacy," *Review for Religious* 34 (February 1975).

5. Keith Clark, *An Experience of Celibacy* (Notre Dame, Ind.: Ave Maria Press, 1982), p. 16.

6. Sidney Callahan, "Personal Growth and Sexuality: Adolescent and Adult Development Stages," *Chicago Studies* 20 (Spring 1981): 19-39.

that the individual be involved in social relationships with others. This process implies constant communication. Normal human life cannot exist without human interaction. For celibates to understand their sexuality, they must interact with persons of both sexes.

There is no doubt that marriage has a profound effect on the emotional life of a man or woman. So does celibacy. The significance of the renunciation of genital sexuality has special meaning for the development of the emotional life. As Rollo May points out, ". . . for human beings, the more powerful need is not for sex per se, but for relationship, intimacy, acceptance and affirmation."[7] And Erik Erikson observes: "Every truly mature man and woman must be capable of experiencing genital sexuality with a mature partner of the opposite sex. However, the same is true for its renunciation."[8] The behavioral sciences and important psychological studies demonstrate that the need is not so much for genitality as for relationships that are either fully masculine or fully feminine.

For centuries the call to celibacy in the Western Church has required and invited human beings to transcend and sublimate genital sexual needs. Although priests and religious do have unconscious motivations, their conscious vocational goal is the fulfillment of a spiritual need based on Christian values. Today priests and religious are encouraged to develop human relationships as a sign of their deep and mysterious relationship with Christ.

Celibacy as a way of life is meaningful only if it is a way of loving. It says something about a person's relationship to God only to the degree that it says something significant about human relationships. We priests and religious relate as body persons to other body persons. We are called to integral emotional relationships because the Christ by whom we are called is human as well as divine. God calls us because of our humanity and not

7. Rollo May, *Love and Will* (New York: W. W. Norton, 1969).

8. Thomas A. Kane, *Who Controls Me?* (Hicksville, N.Y.: Exposition—Collegium Books, 1974).

in spite of it. The vitality of celibate witness can couple the negation of genitality with affirmation of other human beings and open us to receiving their affirmation.[9]

Eschatological witness means little if the celibate's life is not a meaningful affirmation of his or her sexuality in the world. Jesus did not purchase his purity by removing himself from men and women but rather by being involved with them. Further, the Resurrection affirms for humanity the active presence of Christ, as a man, fully man, with manhood purchased not by simple negation but by affirmation of his humanity—an affirmation repeated in word and deed over and over again in the Gospel accounts.

2. *The value of man-woman relationships*

Eugene Kennedy reminds us that it is sexual fascism to force people into a belief system where full humanness is impossible without the gratification of the genital drive. The celibate proclaimers give great value to the development of relationships. My colleague Brother Doctor Martin Helldorfer, F.S.C., reminds us in his essay elsewhere in this book and in a previous paper[10] that there is an inescapable conflict in direction between life as a celibate and the cultivation and expression of genital love. To opt for the celibate way of life means that love for another person will be nongenital in its expression, but it does not mean that the love will be less intimate.

The question of genital or nongenital relationships is not one of loving or not loving, but of allowing the question itself to surface. Sometimes the question is hardly given a chance to do so. For example, our words hold back the question. We speak of chaste love as nonexclusive. But this idea is almost incomprehensible to persons in love because they see clearly that it is the exclusive aspect of a relationship that distinguishes it as such.

---

9. Thomas A. Kane, *Happy Are You Who Affirm* (Whitinsville, Mass.: Affirmation Books, 1980).

10. Martin Helldorfer, "Genital Relationships: A Question of Integrity," in *Sexuality* (Lockport, Ill.: Christian Brothers' Conference, 1977), pp. 61-63.

Sometimes our attitudes hold back the question of what happens to celibates who fall in love. We may give the impression that things are not as they should be. However, the persons involved in the relationship do not view the experience of loving and being loved as something wrong. They feel strongly that it is, on the contrary, a blessing. Brother Martin goes on to explain that obscuring the question of how to love and forcing the relationship underground privatizes the relationship and heightens the intensity of sexual feelings, moving the ones who love toward marital love.

The celibate proclaimer bears witness to the value of loving in a way that does not necessarily lead to genital love. The growth of this kind of love involves learning to relate in ways that open new areas of intimacy, highlighting the rich emotional value of self-restraining love. Deeply rooted in reality, we must take account of our biological, psychological, and spiritual selves. Human relationships require time and space. We need time because we are talking about growth; we need space to create an open atmosphere that prevents the love relationship from becoming private. We can be sure that relating in love will not remove the desire for genital expression; however, the movement toward nongenital love must itself be an expression of love for another if it is to last.

The celibate's proclamation of relationship is a statement to Church and society that there is a grace involved in falling in love with another person. Loving and being loved deepen our understanding of the futility of life without love. We are awakened to a gentleness not only toward others but also toward ourselves. This gentle compassion brings us to the heart of the Christian life—certainly, a tremendous grace.

3. *The value of the reflective life*

The celibate proclaimer lives a life that is reflective rather than reactive. Meaningful celibacy is a conversion experience that is not caught up in defining life in general as doing, or in categorizing people by what they do. Rather, the emphasis is on being. Time and space are given to a life style that is not just another form of utilitarian workaholism but rather an experience of reflection, meditation, and prayer, of taking time to see beauty and to smell the rose. The celibate proclaimer does not escape hard work, but puts it in its proper place. The Eucharist is the center of the proclaimer's valuing of reflection, and the celebration of the Real Presence is seen in sacrament and in person.

Living a reflective life, the celibate proclaimers raise humanity's level of consciousness with regard to the urgency of the Kingdom of God. These celibates as a society of men and women living and loving in Christ consecrate themselves entirely to the preparation of that Kingdom. As they work for the liberation of each person and an experience that will reconcile that person to God, the celibate proclaimers make Christ's love visible and bear witness to the Kingdom. When this happens a new kind of human relationship can be established.

4. *The value of living life dangerously*

Celibate proclaimers cultivate a life style that allows risk, initiative, and taking a stand. Sister Anna Polcino, religious, surgeon, and psychiatrist, has often used the expression "to live life dangerously." In her own work among the people of Pakistan and Bangladesh as well as in her founding of the House of Affirmation, she offers testimony that the celibate may frequently be called to a prophetic position, even to taking an unpopular stand.[11] Of course, I am not referring here to masochistic behavior, but rather to a generosity that aligns itself with the physically, emotionally, or spiritually poor among us.

The celibate proclaimers are not willing merely to maintain the status quo; on the contrary, they are committed to the liberation of all people. Thus today we see bishops in the United States taking a strong stand against nuclear weapons and warfare; we witness the martyrdom of the holy women in El Salvador; and we hear a pope speak about the rights of the workers.

---

11. Anna Polcino, *Loneliness: The Genesis of Solitude, Friendship, and Contemplation* (Whitinsville, Mass.: Affirmation Books, 1979).

Karl Rahner in his essay on the future of the Church points out how necessary it is to have a "world view" rather than merely a national or local view in our evangelization.[12] Celibate proclaimers are often able to facilitate this world view in their service, at the same time keeping alive the urgency of the needs of all people.

The celibate proclaimers speak loudly today about the ambiguous position of women in the Church. On the one hand, women exercise many important functions in the Church; on the other, they are denied all official ministries, ordained and non-ordained. The proclaimers remind us that the time has come to face this situation seriously and to recognize the validity of ministry for women in the Church. The exigencies of the present time, both in the world at large and in many local churches, demand such a recognition. There is a growing awareness of the equality of women in all spheres, and of their specific roles in human society. The call experienced by many women to dedicate themselves to the service of others in various ministries has had serious repercussions on discussions regarding ministry in the Church. Women are full members of the Church. Discrimination against them on the basis of sex will deny to the Church their particular gifts and charisms. Although the question of the admission of women to the priesthood demands further historical and theological research, their induction into all other ministries has the backing of both theology and tradition. The presence of women in a variety of ministries will also lead to new dimensions of team ministry and to a progressive change in the self-image of priests and religious. The celibate proclaimers promote steps to prepare both men and women for the time when women share in the ministry of the Church. This development will not minimize the charism of institutes of religious women but will enable their particular gifts to be even more fruitful through the ministrations of their sisters.

---

12. Karl Rahner, "Planning the Church of the Future," *Theology Digest* 30 (Spring 1982): 59-62.

The celibate proclaimers often take on the position of encouraging the full dignity of the role of the laity in the Church. Vatican II documents reminded the people of God that the laity have special gifts, rooted in baptism, that are manifestations of the Spirit. The documents are an invitation to translate into actual practice the conviction that the responsibility of the Church in her mission to the world cannot be borne by clergy and religious alone. This responsibility must be shared by all Christians through a distribution of tasks and functions.

5. *The value of sacrifice*

The celibate proclaimers point to the reality that there is something more to life than just self-fulfillment. Aware of their own integration and maturity, they are able to go beyond mere self-interests. Today there is so much talk about self-realization, self-actualization, self-this, and self-that that one may begin to believe that the world is supposed to serve the individual rather than the reverse.

The ministry of service often calls for a delay in personal gratification that can lead one to a fuller maturity through service to others. The same attitude that led Christ to empty himself of all his rights and to become obedient even to death on the cross will lead celibates to die to their own selfishness by participating—receiving and giving—in a community of love. These men and women are able to experience how emotionally enriching giving to others can be because they have first learned to receive.

Some may contend that the celibate proclaimers are but a small group, perhaps even an ideal that does not exist. I know they have existed from centuries past and are here among us today. I do not know their number, but I do know that they offer us an example of how to live the celibate ideal with human compassion firmly rooted in friendship with Christ.

The Grumpies

Henri Nouwen uses the following term, which I find particularly apt, to describe some people in ministry: "the grumpy children of God." Father Pable points out that these grumpy children of God are often suffering from "low-key hostility."

They are not openly angry people; they are quietly and passively bitter. They resent the burdens of celibacy, the ineptness of religious leadership, the confusion of theology, and the ingratitude of the faithful.

The roots of the grumpies' problem may be much deeper than celibacy and may have their origin more in the sociological and cultural atmosphere of contemporary society. Many of these celibates have the empty feeling of being strangers to themselves. Feeling nonaffirmed, they go about their duties as priests or religious in a manner that witnesses much more to rugged individualism, emotional retardation, and social ineptness than to the warm vitality and compassion of Christ.

However, we must not be too quick to judge the grumpies; rather, we need to minister to them, to invite them to personal renewal, to gentleness with themselves, to growing compassion toward their own self-expectations, the results of which will flow into the lives of the people they serve. In *Spiritual Renewal of the American Priesthood*, E. Larkin and G. Broccolo remind us that "it is a cruel suffering to feel useless, out of date, not needed, rejected; to experience the conflict of having to preach a Gospel the people do not want to hear."[13]

Support Systems

All celibates, but in particular our grumpy brothers and sisters, need support systems made up of priests, religious, and laity. Larkin and Broccolo emphasize this fact with regard to the American priesthood, but their point applies to religious as well.

> The American priest needs others—his bishop, his brother priests and those with whom he shares a deep faith—to provide personal interest and perhaps actual presence in his prayer life. Left alone he can too easily crawl into the hole his guilts have dug for him. Left alone, he can easily divorce his prayer life from his ministerial activity. Left alone, he does not have

---

13. E. Larkin and G. Broccolo, *Spiritual Renewal of the American Priesthood* (Washington, D.C.: National Conference of Catholic Bishops, 1972), p. 20.

the usual instrument the Lord uses to sharpen and purify faith, namely, a community of faith.[14]

Intimacy

I believe the awkwards, the proclaimers, and the grumpies are in the race—some graciously, some not so graciously—toward the intimacy with their God and neighbor that celibacy calls forth. Yet another group of celibates, to whom I have not even alluded, are the *undisciplined*—those who do not care about any Church tradition, charism, or invitation. They live uninfluenced by the Christian community and do just what they please. These people are not striving toward intimacy but rather are often on the path to self-destruction.

Conclusion

The following quote, from *The Shoes of the Fisherman,* nicely sums up the celibate renunciation: to proclaim again a creature's romance with the creator.

> To meet a whole man is an ennobling experience. It costs so much to be a full human being that there are very few who have the enlightenment or the courage to pay the price. One has to abandon altogether the search for security and reach out to embrace the world like a lover, and yet demand no easy return of love. One has to accept pain as a condition of existence. One has to court doubt and darkness as the cost of knowing. One needs a will stubborn in conflict but apt always to the total acceptance of every consequence of living and dying.
>
> . . . If a man is centered upon himself, the smallest risk is too great for him because both success and failure can destroy him. If he is centered upon God, then no risk is too great, because success is already guaranteed—the successful union of Creator and creature, beside which everything else is meaningless.[15]

---

14. Ibid, p. 34.

15. Morris West, *The Shoes of the Fisherman* (New York: William Morrow, 1963), pp. 255, 365.

Audrey E. Campbell-Wray, Ph.D., director of education for the House of Affirmation, has graduate degrees in theology from St. John's University, New York, and in applied spirituality from the University of San Francisco. She received her master's and doctoral degrees in clinical psychology from the Psychological Studies Institute in Palo Alto, California. Dr. Campbell-Wray is a psychotherapist, art therapist, and spiritual director, and has conducted numerous workshops and retreats on issues of psychological and spiritual health and growth. She is a member of several professional organizations including the American Psychological Association and the American Art Therapy Association.

Relating to the Ugly:
Shadows and Grandiosity

Audrey E. Campbell-Wray

Relating to the Ugly when the heart is not enough
to teach the mind compassion
Is a nearly impossible task.
We would reject the pain
   and the awful, awful truth.
Compassion gleans the best of both.
Relating to the Ugly.
The task is to summon courage
And wade, wade through. Enormous courage, a world of
courage, borrowed courage, latent courage, courage from
anyone, courage from anywhere.
It is a moral, ethical, social, psychological, and profoundly
spiritual task.
Relating the the Ugly.
To embrace the awful, awful truth
and hold the awful pain. Drawing them closer with
commitment to the darkness as our wretchedness reveals
itself. We'd like to take the wretched out of Amazing
Grace. But the awful, awful lingering demands the awful,
awful truth.
Wretched walking, wretched talking
All wretched. Wretch and clear.
No, it lingers. Lingers because
It *must* be *loved. Relate* to the *Ugly*!

The Shadow

It is a very large and beautiful basilica-kind of building, with only one large circular stained-glass window high in the rear that appears to be a very intricate mandala design. The ceiling is high enough to be in heaven but is dimly lit. The rows and rows of pews surrounded and bounded and formed by aisles and pillars are placed a respectful distance away from the royal sanctuary, which is marked less by the inconsequential altar than by the life-size corpus crucified on a cross suspended by chains beneath an elaborate balustrade. But he appears somewhat peaceful hanging there, and approachable should you decide to enter upon a colloquy. It is an appealing place when the dark pillars and the dark walls and the dim lights engulf an empty space, so silent that a footstep echoes, a dropped coin resounds, and one can almost hear the candle flames flicker.

Such a place was new and magic: I had been a Catholic a mere matter of months and few of them at that. I did not remember things like holy days of obligation, but this was one. So I raced toward the church on my lunch hour, expecting to assume my hidden post in this dark, sober, silent haven of peace. But everywhere there were busy, moving people milling about. There was a hum of activity—now some singing, now some shifting of positions—while in the background that deep monotonal, hypnotic repetition of "Body of Christ," "Body of Christ," "Body of Christ."

I moved to the rear and wiggled my way into a crowded pew. The many people with their faithful faces and folded fingers had a mystique all their own. But I was not interested in joining in; I waited anxiously, in fact, for the liturgy to quickly end and the people to quickly leave so that the dark and silent, mystical atmosphere might return to my basilica. Thus, I knelt in the pew and fixed my attention on that mammoth crucifix which suddenly seemed to expand, explode to the fullest extent of my consciousness. Everything and everyone else receded. The body of Christ seemed to loose itself from the cross, bending toward me as if to whisper a secret. He spoke without moving his face or lips, and the word spoken was "love," "love," "love"; it reverberated repetitiously as he gradually resumed his former position, crucified on the cross. It took me a much longer time to resume my former composure. I dashed across two lawns to where paper and pen awaited my frantic recording, stuffed it into an envelope, and mailed it off to a priest friend in Canada. Then it suddenly occurred to me that he might think me a stark raving lunatic.

"Love" is what He said. It is that disarmed, vulnerable, out-stretched stance in the world that is as strong as death as noted in the Song of Songs. There was *no pain* in that encounter. There was something incredibly good. There was *no negativity*. Saint Ignatius of Loyola in his work on the Spiritual Exercises speaks of this as "consolation without a cause"—an encounter with the divine touch so totally sweet, pure, and transforming that it is the only human experience totally free of negativity. It can never be duplicated or undone. It becomes knowledge; granted, a unique way of knowing, but it is a certain knowledge that encounters difficulty in verbalization. Yet it is the kind of experience that people have attempted to communicate for centuries.

"Love" of what? Of whom? Of crucifixion, of communion rituals, of me, of death, of all the faithful little people, of my comforting basilica, of mysteries I cannot understand? What message did he intend to convey? That the whole shebang, everything that is, is because of love? That in the end even all of the Jungian opposites can be gathered up into love? That in the eschatological season eternity might mean union without destruction? That the powerful love of the returning Christ might unify all opposites, so that the creatures will no longer need to liberate energy through conflict? That the transforming power of love will energize—as it does in the Godhead?

It is so in the image of the sun. The sun carries no shadow in itself; it is always the sun. It has no obstruction within it, just as within the Trinity there is no negativity. If the moon represents the first half of life, characterized by the problems of the shadow, the anima, and the animus, the sun represents the second half of life, characterized by transit, perhaps soaring into cosmic consciousness. The sun never stops shining; only its light can be hidden, as in an eclipse when the moon comes between the shining sun and our eyes. If we stand between the moon shadow of our daily labor and problems and the sun's pure light, noting the power and reality of both, we are energized by the struggle, by the conflict. It is probably also true that we would find ourselves immobile were we aware of one and not the other. This is assuming that there are so few of us energized by the power of love alone that the struggle is passé and the conflict no longer raging. The struggle is the normal way of passage toward the light. It seems to have much to do with our necessary freedom to make moral choices, as we would otherwise be a race of robots. We seem to have to choose progressively to face the daily toil, to face the shadow, to face the conflict, to face the light. It requires an intense commitment to one's own truth, to one's own passion. And it is exemplified in the life of Christ.

Carl Jung's transcendent function is at the center of the cross. The significance of the center is the Gem. Moving along a path between two opposing forces, the center is a highly energized position, for in the concept of enantiodromia, the one is constantly flowing into the other. It is perceived as conflict in my subjective experience, and the gift of the pain is the struggle for definition, resolution, meaning, and self-definition, or else there would be only neurotic attachment to ongoing pain. But, in the center of the squared circle, there resides the possibility of integration, wholeness, of all essential meanings. The possibility of integration, you understand, but for some there is also the experience of flight. Here again within this flight the opposites flow into one another, toward something and away from something—perhaps away from the confused and empty sense of identity, but toward a great many endeavors, creativity, and achievements. "Jung's concept is that the aim of one's life, psychologically speaking, should be not to suppress or repress, but to come to know one's other side, and so both to enjoy and to control the whole range of one's capacities."[1]

---

1. Joseph Campbell, ed., *The Portable Jung* (New York: Viking Press, 1971), p. xxvii.

Jung's transcendent function is at the center of the cross. The four beams represent the pairs of faculties: sensation and intuition, feeling and thinking. If you turn your back on one it will sneak up on you, approaching from the rear—moving toward its opposite. Individuation is the process of achieving sufficient control of all four faculties to enable a vision of transcendence, movement into the unknown.

Leaning too exclusively on our frantic grasping for the light leaves our backs quite vulnerable to the approaching shadow. The shadow must be faced, confronted, and waded through. There is a Gem in the center.

The shadow becomes a repository for the truth that we cannot own and cannot bear and cannot integrate due to early trauma, developmental blocks, and inappropriately unempathic care.

The shadow is not to be equated with death. What kills is the lack of courage and the lack of choosing to turn, confront, and learn to hold and nurture the awful pain and the awful truth. Relate to the Ugly.

Grandiosity and Idealization

Consider now the fragile, aching person whose fear is that confrontation with the shadow will confirm his or her self-hatred and dread.

You have met those strained and aching persons who so fear their inner pain that they seek to convince you of their perfection in everything and in every way. They can ferret out a slight from the most mundane of interactions. It is an alertness to protect themselves from the conniving of all other human beings to confirm their own self-hatred, or so their psyches think. They are quick to judge others stupid or unkind, thus helping to maintain their sense of being right. They need order and control, control, and more control. They are fearful of intimacy and usually unable to sustain relationships over time. They are constantly seeking *the ideal* and needing but rarely asking for praise and encouragement. They are often in dire need of holding, nurturing, and loving, and at the same time find it almost impossible to place themselves in a receiving mode. Their gifts and talents may be obvious, even overwhelming, to others, but their inner experience is that their ambitions, goals, and ideals are never met. They will rage when their imperfections are revealed. They will curse the revealer, hate themselves, wish they were dead, and experience a sense of hopelessness that is difficult to comprehend.

Let us consider Heinz Kohut's model of the bipolar self.

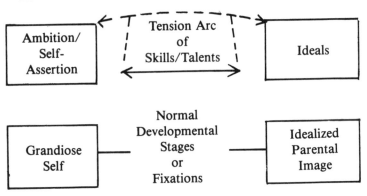

The grandiose self represents that pole at which the developing child needs to be flooded with esteem, praise, joy, and delight. "O my precious little one, that picture you painted is the best ever. See, I hung it on the wall"; and "You are a very good person." A phase of self-infatuation is appropriate as the child learns delight in his or her very being. Healthy development at the idealized parental image pole requires the consistent empathic relationship of the parental figure. The parent needs to stay on the pedestal, that is, to stay empathic enough to be idealized by the child, long enough for the child to internalize the admired ideals. Some parental figures may fail to aid healthy development at these poles through abandonment, chronic illness, abuse, alcoholism, or chronic inability to treat each child as a separate, unique person who exists in his or her own right.

The bipolar self is the root of *self psychology*. The goal is a healthy, *cohesive* inner self.

> The self, the core of our personality, has various constituents
> which we acquire in the interplay with those persons in our

earliest childhood environment whom we experience as self-objects. A firm self, resulting from the optimal interactions between the child and his self-objects is made up of three major constituents: (1) one pole from which emanate the basic strivings for power and success; (2) another pole that harbours the basic idealized goals; and (3) an intermediate area of basic talents and skills that are activated by the tension-arc that establishes itself between ambitions and ideals.[2]

The cohesive nuclear self is formed by the deeply anchored, phase appropriate responsiveness of those significant others. It is empathic nurturance in a growth-producing sense that allows dependency and eventual freedom, merging and eventual self-definition.

An unhealthy fearful perfectionism demands the view that everything good is inside or just like me and everything bad is outside or different. Gone awry the grandiose self can lead to a religious fanaticism, or to fanatic nationalism, or to prejudice. If the early relationship fails at the idealized parent pole, there may ensue a lifelong search for an idol, a guru, an ideal person, God. The chronically poorly-nurtured person may come to believe that the human environment is basically inimical; and that the human God is basically punitive and unable to be satisfied.

A healed and healthy cohesive self allows the maximum acquisition of self-esteem, ego-syntonic pleasure in success, empathy, creativity, humor, and wisdom. Above all, energy is freed for a total love experience. This response can be the result of early empathic parenting, or it can result from the transmuted internalization that comes of working through a narcissistic transference in therapy. One can then be open without the fear of being crushed. It is at this point that men and women can love themselves enough to allow a moment of being wholly and deeply touched by another human being or by God.

---

2. Heinz Kohut and Ernst Wolf, ''The Disorders of the Self and Their Treatment: An Outline,'' *International Journal of Psychoanalysis* 59 (1978): 413-26.

The Compassion of Nurturance

Relating to the Ugly when the heart is not enough
To teach the mind compassion
Is a nearly impossible task.
We would reject the awful, awful pain
And the awful, awful truth.
Compassion gleans the best of both.

It is *appropriate* that you should be loved and empathically nurtured into a healthy, cohesive inner self. It is no small task to accomplish as an adult, and it is not a do-it-yourself project. You must allow me to transmit love and esteem to you; and I must persist in a sometimes quiet, sometimes noisy loving presence until you do.

But before you can receive my love you must begin with members of your own self. Begin with the physical pains and tension-holding locations in your body. Sit and talk with them awhile. Now visualize and bathe them in a warm and gentle light.

Choose the part or whole of your body you hate, or fear, or hate and fear. Now touch, hold, warm, and bathe it as Frederick Leboyer would have the new father touch, hold, warm, and bathe the newborn child.

Speaking of the child—when was the last time you sat your inner child down in a chair and listened to him or her, or held him or her, or gifted him or her with a just-for-fun treat? We are creatures of time and do very little relating without the passage of time together.

Now, let us move to raw feelings. Can you imagine or visualize cradling in your arms your pain, or anger, or longing, or infatuation, or fear? Can you imagine holding Christ's head on your shoulder—and your love and compassion being enough?

We are ready to come back now to your receiving my love and esteem for you.

I am the person whom you fear most
                                hate most
                                find most different
                                find most annoying.

And I am loving you with my passion in my own peculiar way.
Relate to the Ugly.

I am the person whom you bomb in war

> fear on the streets
> see drunk on the subway
> see hungry in the desert.

And I would love you with my passion in my own peculiar
way—if you came close enough to touch. Relate to the Ugly.

"The Oath"

I promise to do my duty,
To love you each and every day
In big and little (sometimes practically nonexistent) ways.
I pledge allegiance to your *ugliness* and commitment to our
relationship provided that the awful truth and awful pain
are not excluded. I know there is a Gem in the center of
all of this Ugly.
P.S. I forgive God.

Conclusion

Not even centuries of symbolic language and experience make
clear to us all the mysteries of creation nor all the meanings of
our own experience. Though we get bogged down in words and
dogmas, many of us continue to record our experiences of a God
of Pure Light and no negativity. I cannot escape the reality of
my own negativity; nor the adversity posed by the "principalities
and powers" of darkness, as Paul expressed it, that is outside of
my own contributions; nor a savior who walks the Via Dolorosa
—the way of suffering.

I also cannot escape my understanding of the Lord of love and
impenetrable light, nor the rich religious symbolism and ritual
that corroborate that inner experience.

Let the first thing that I learn from Papa Jung be that fierce
integrity and moral courage to walk upon the two-edged sword
of my own passion and avoid nothing that compels from within
—to admit all possibilities, mythical, historical, psychological,
and spiritual as I chisel in the stone.

Once upon a time, there was a very bright and alert little boy who skipped along the streets of a busy European town on his way to and from school. Even though his feet moved swiftly, his eyes steadily engaged the familiar and the new. The mysterious sculptor's shop with its wide window, curious forms, and huge block of marble did not escape him. It was one of his favorite places to stop. He would press his face against the glass and peer in. Gradually, and to his complete amazement, he began to notice that the form of the marble block was changing. Though it did so ever so slowly, the boy now never failed to stop daily to see what had happened overnight. For months and months, day after day he would look, and day after day there was ever so little change. Finally, one morning, he stopped, pressed his face against the glass, and found himself so entirely astonished that he forgot he had been on his way to school. He stood wide-eyed for such a long time that the sculptor finally noticed him and beckoned him to enter. He entered. He circled the magnificent animal that stood where the block of marble had previously been, then turned breathlessly to the sculptor and asked: "How did you know that that lion was hidden in the stone?"

And the Gem is in the heart of the lion.

Reverend John A. Struzzo, C.S.C., Ph.D., is a full-time psychotherapist at the House of Affirmation in Montara, California. A priest of the Congregation of Holy Cross, Fr. Struzzo received his bachelor's and master's degrees in theology and sociology at the University of Notre Dame and his doctorate in sociology from Florida State University. For several years Fr. Struzzo was Professor of Sociology at Northern Illinois University. He then completed a postgraduate certificate in marriage and family psychotherapy at the Institute of Religion and Health in New York City, and interned in clinical psychology at Worcester State Hospital. Before joining the staff of the House of Affirmation, Fr. Struzzo was executive director of a pastoral counseling center in South Bend, Indiana. He has lectured widely on issues relating to psychology and religion, and on personal growth and development. He is a member of the American Association of Pastoral Counselors, the American Association of Marriage and Family Therapists, and the California Association of Marriage and Family Therapy.

Intimate Relationships:
Heterosexual and Homosexual

John A. Struzzo

When we think of intimacy, we usually also think of sexuality. Although sexuality and intimacy can be considered distinct entities, they are also directly related to each other. I am presupposing that a mature psychosexual development is a prerequisite for intimate relations of any depth. By its very nature sexuality is a longing to surrender to something bigger than oneself and a desire for union, as well as being the source of one's creative potential. Thus to deny or repress one's sexuality is basically to stifle one's ability to become intimate.

Celibacy is a way of sexual loving manifest in a genuine and integrated experience of intimacy, which expresses qualities that are basic to ministry, such as gentleness, compassion, sensitivity, and warmth. I would argue that intimacy with God for celibates is mirrored in their intimacy with their fellow men and women, and with themselves. Furthermore, intimacy in relationships involves the total person—body, sexuality, mind, emotions, and spirit. Thus sexuality, intimacy, celibacy, and union with God are interdependent and interconnected.

How does one grow toward a mature psychosexual intimacy? What is the specific relationship of the celibate to that process? In what way is the particular situation of the homosexual relevant? Lastly, how do community structures affect that process of growth? These are the questions I will address in this chapter.

Immature Psychosexual Intimacy

Immaturity in intimate relationships is rooted in the deprivation and repression of basic needs. Its basic premise is, I need you, therefore I love you. Mature intimacy has for its basic thesis, I love you, therefore I need you. The example of climbing a tree can help us understand this difference.[1] I can climb a tree to test my strength or to get a better view. I can also climb a tree because I am being chased by a wild animal. In the first instance, my motive for climbing is pleasure. In the second, I am motivated by fear and the need for safety. In the former case I am free to climb or not. Thus I can be discriminate and look for the tree best suited to my purpose. However, in the second example, I feel compelled by necessity and indiscriminately climb the first tree in sight.

Mature intimacy is like climbing the tree for pleasure. The predominant feeling is affection. In immature intimacy, the need for reassurance is primary. I feel driven by anxiety and my needs, and thus tend to be compulsive and indiscriminate in my choice of object. I am like a starving person who will eat any food. For example, let us suppose I am starving for affection and go to the bank to cash a check. While doing so, I perceive the teller as being attractive, and she smiles at me. If I am immature, I may feel I am in love, whereas a mature person would experience the teller as friendly but not read anything else into the transaction. Likewise, if I have come to like someone and that person does not smile, I will tend to feel hurt and rejected. Because of my strong need for affection, I want constant proof of others' approval. The need for acceptance seems insatiable.[2]

Underlying immature intimacy is the assumption that there is someone out there who will take care of me, who will right all wrongs and protect me from danger. One tends to live in unconscious illusion of a fairy-tale existence, expecting fulfillment and happiness to come from others. Such an assumption masks

---

1. Karen Horney, *The Neurotic Personality of Our Time* (New York: W. W. Norton, 1937), pp. 103-104.

2. Ibid., pp. 104-105.

one's true feelings of helplessness, fear, anger and confusion, and brings false hope to a chaotic life. It prevents struggling with ethical ideals and the limits of imperfect situations, which is the basis of growth. Thus both personal and spiritual growth are hindered.

When people feel needy and deprived of love, they mistake their experience of neediness for love itself. When affection is offered, such persons meet it with distrust and disbelief. They do not trust it, because they believe they are unlovable; and they refuse to accept it, because they believe the love is offered for ulterior motives. You love me because it is your job to do so, or because you want something from me, or because I forced you to.

Yet, since getting affection is so important, needy men and women will pay any price for it. The most common price is an attitude of emotional dependency and compliance.[3] They fear criticizing or disagreeing, and show only loyalty and docility. The approval of others is constantly sought, and at the same time great resentment builds up over having to be so pleasing. The personality manifestations of such neediness are passive-dependent and passive-aggressive types, which in my experience seem so common among clergy and religious.

Passive people are so busy seeking love that there is little energy left to love others. They feel like a bottomless, unfillable pit. Because of the strength of this sense of inner emptiness and hunger for affection, it is difficult to postpone gratification.[4] The focus of energy is, how can I get others to take care of my needs? If the other is a caretaker type of personality, needy persons tend to feel that at last their needs will be met, and their loneliness will be taken away. But they quickly become bored and disappointed because they drain the other of the little variety he or she has to offer. They then tend to rationalize that the relationship offers no future, and blame the other for their own failure and feelings of inadequacy.

---

3. Ibid., pp. 119-20.

4. Ibid., pp. 124-34.

Because of their fear of rejection, immature people become lost in an endless preoccupation with a search for self-confirmation in others.[5] At the same time, they hope they do not find what they want, for then commitment would be demanded of them. Since the clinging and frantic attachment to others constricts and traps them, they ultimately drive the other person away and destroy the relationship. Their main concern is not the growth of the other, but whether the other will be there to satisfy their needs. Noncompliance with their wishes is experienced as rejection. Thus changes in appointments, periods of having to wait, or disagreements with their opinions are interpreted as personal rejections, which increases their basic anxiety. The more anxious they become, the more clinging and possessive. Thus the process becomes a vicious circle.[6]

Genital Intimacy and Immaturity

Sex as Human Contact

Sex frequently becomes an inappropriate catchall for unmet love needs. One may become genitally involved because one has never experienced intimacy with anyone on any level, including parents and friends. Thus a person can translate a simple desire to be loved into a desire to be genitally intimate. For some people, genital relations are the only way they know to get human contact. Physical contact can become a substitute for emotional relationships. Although they become genitally intimate, what they find satisfying is the physical closeness. If sexuality is the only bridge leading to contact with others, it acquires abnormal importance.[7]

---

5. Allan Fromme, *The Ability to Love* (New York: Pocket Books, 1971), p. 142.

6. John F. Crosby, *Illusion and Delusion* (Belmont, Calif.: Wadsworth, 1973), pp. 21-36; Horney, *The Neurotic Personality,* pp. 102-46; Fromme, *The Ability to Love,* pp. 141-57.

7. Horney, *The Neurotic Personality,* pp. 153-54.

Sex as Reassurance

Much of what appears as sexuality is in reality the expression of a need for reassurance. Males who have doubts about their masculinity, for example, may use sex to demonstrate their sexual prowess. Likewise, some women use sex to reassure themselves that they are desirable and to confirm that they are lovable. The problem is that when sex is used for reassurance, the root of the inadequacy, which motivates the need in the first place, remains untouched.[8]

Sex as Energizer

For many people life is boring and devoid of satisfaction, so they engage in sexual relations as a compensation for the emptiness of their lives. Although sex can temporarily alleviate the pain of boredom and loneliness, the emptiness remains. Frequently such people feel disillusioned and even more lonely afterward.[9]

Sex as Exchange

Another way immature people use sex is to attempt to buy affection. Such a use is dehumanizing because the participants are reduced to commodities. Sex cannot create intimacy when there is no closeness or affection to begin with. Often, sexual expression without intimacy violates one's own personal needs and values, and leads to feelings of guilt and frustration.[10]

Sex as Conquest or Punishment

Sometimes sex and anger become so inextricably linked that a sadomasochistic relationship seems in reality motivated by one and the same intrapsychic dynamic. In my clinical experience counseling people in sadomasochistic relationships, two patterns appear prevalent. First, there is a family history of physical and verbal abuse. Second, the client uses strong intellectual defenses

---

8. Bernie Zilbergeld, *Male Sexuality* (New York: Bantam Books, 1978), pp. 358-64.

9. Ibid., pp. 364-67.

10. Ibid., p. 367.

and feels emotionally dead. The obverse of pain is passion. In the sadomasochistic relationship, the pain becomes so intense that it breaks through the intellectual defenses. Thus this kind of relationship is an attempt to deal with anger toward an abusing parent, as well as a way to feel alive. I have also observed in my clinical experience that repressed anger can lead to sexual impotence, as well as impotence in general.

In all the above issues of sex, there is a sexualization of basic needs of security, power, and affection, as well as the confusion of sex with anger and love. Sexual expression in the immature person also tends to be compulsive and indiscriminate. Underlying the sexual behaviors are often psychic tensions and anxiety rather than a true sexual drive or need.

Sex often becomes a defense against involvement for immature people; it is used to escape from an uncomfortable situation or feeling. When sex is not the goal but is used to satisfy other goals and needs, impersonal contact is the likely result. It offers the appearance of human contact without the problems that real contact and intimacy entail. In some ways, sex is easier than talking or eye contact. Thus sex can be a way to avoid communication and vulnerability, which are the basis of mature intimacy.[11]

Repression and Sexuality

Sexual feelings and desires are the roots of intimacy and tenderness.[12] In the preceding discussion of the sexualization of human needs, I argued that for the immature person, sexual expression can be a compensatory behavior for intimacy deprivation. Another way immature people may cope with sexual feelings and desires is to repress them. People who repress their sexuality are generally unable to express care or affection, and

---

11. Ibid., pp. 368-73.

12. Thomas J. Tyrrell, *Urgent Longings: Reflections on the Experience of Infatuation, Human Intimacy, and Contemplative Love* (Whitinsville, Mass.: Affirmation Books, 1980), p. 50.

when they attempt to do so, it is without real warmth or tenderness. They are unable to become intimate.[13]

We are present to others through our bodies. Repressed people are absent and inaccessible. Unconsciously, they deny and disown their sexual feelings. When they do experience them, they perceive them as bad and alien. Not only are sexual feelings cut off but aliveness in general. There is a feeling of inner emptiness, under which is often a depression. However, such people frequently are not aware of their lack of aliveness. They have become so accustomed to thinking of the body as a tool of the mind that they accept its relative deadness as a normal state.[14] Such people tend to be aware of only pain, fear, sadness, and anger. Joy, spontaneity, and pleasure are not allowed, and are beyond awareness. In disowning their sexual feelings they cease to experience them. They may experience muscular tension, especially in the pelvic area, which numbs them so they can no longer feel their inner state. Often they express their repressed sexuality by becoming overweight or anorexic. But more than simply sexual feelings become blocked. Positive feelings in general, and especially the capacity to experience pleasure, are diminished. Since the ability to experience pleasure is a sustaining creative force in our lives, such people tend to be lonely and unhappy, empty and lifeless.[15]

To escape this inner emptiness, repressed people often escape into workaholism or oral abuses such as alcoholism, overeating, or oversmoking, or into promiscuous genital behavior. Repressed sex and sexual promiscuity are simply two sides of the same coin, except that a person who is sexually active may be more available for growth in intimacy and maturity.

---

13. Ibid.

14. Ibid., pp. 51-4.

15. Alexander Lowen, *Pleasure* (New York: Lancer Books, 1970), p. 24.

The Psychosexual Celibate

Celibacy and Repressed Sexuality

The basic motive for celibacy is to transform sexual energy into a higher union of love. However, if we try to control sexual energy without first coming to know it, it will turn against us. We cannot destroy sexual energy; we can only transform or release it. If we never come to know and experience it, it will be thrust into the unconscious and manifest itself in physical and emotional disorders.[16] Thus, to let go of sexuality in order to transform it into a celibate intimacy and love assumes one was first in possession of it.

We can let go of sexual needs and desires only after we first have experienced and accepted ourselves as sexual. If we believe that as a result of celibacy, we are missing out on something, then the focus will be not on letting go and transforming sexuality, but on deprivation. If our primary perception of celibacy is one of sacrifice, then we will feel irritable and place expectations on God. Thus we might feel entitled to material possessions or power for the sacrifice we have made. If control of sex is the focus, then we are simply increasing our sexual energies and contributing to a negative sexual fulfillment.

The attempt to control and ultimately to repress sex suggests a basic fear of sex. Although fear tends to push us to withdraw from the dreaded object, we are also fascinated by what we fear. Thus the fear of sex is in reality an unconscious desire for sex. To use our energy to avoid sex or to repress it is not much different from an addictive and compulsive desire to gratify sexual needs. Aversion and attachment are two sides of the same coin. In other words, abstinence does not necessarily indicate a celibate commitment. Priests or religious who deny their sexuality and compensate for it by overworking, or by surrounding themselves with material objects, or by engaging in various forms of oral abuse may be less celibate than their counterparts who are genitally involved but who are struggling toward

16. Elizabeth Haich, *Sexual Energy and Yoga* (New York: Asi Publishers, 1972), pp. 55-61.

abstinence from genital expression as a personal value and goal. Such a judgment assumes celibacy is a developmental process which attempts to transform sexual energy into an intimate union with God, with others, and with oneself. By denying and trying to root out sexual feelings and desires, the repressed person also roots out the potential for celibate intimacy and therefore union with God. Ultimately the goal of celibacy is not sexual control but a true desire for God.

Celibacy and Psychosexual Maturity

Psychosexual maturity first of all assumes that one is able to acknowledge and experience and accept his or her sexuality without denial and guilt. For the celibate there is the added dimension of being able to pursue intimacy without motivation for genital union.

When one is psychosexually mature, intimate relations are direct, honest, and nonmanipulative. Thus if one expresses physical intimacy through touching or kissing, it is an expression of warmth and affection and not a covert maneuver to incite physical arousal in oneself or in one's partner. Mature people love individuals, not abstract humanity. Such people can be intimate with persons of both sexes without domination, possessiveness, or jealousy. For mature people, intimate relationships are rooted in their awareness of their own body, sexuality, mind, emotions, and spirit. They experience harmony and integration among their thoughts, feelings, values, and behavior. In general, mature people are able to commit themselves to values, cope with value conflicts, and assume responsibility for their choices. Mature celibates hold celibacy as a positive value and experience it as a positive commitment rather than as a rule to which they acquiesce. By owning and integrating their sexuality, psychosexually mature celibates are able to enter into deep, intimate, and loving relationships with both sexes as well as with themselves and with God.

Growth toward Mature Psychosexual Intimacy

If intimacy is essential to human growth and celibate commitment, how does one attain a mature psychosexual intimacy in relationships? If one has repressed his or her sexuality and is already finally professed or ordained, what options are available?

Both sexually repressed and sexually promiscuous men and women usually disown and distrust their sexual feelings, and in general are uncomfortable with their sexuality. Thus the first task of growth toward psychosexual maturity is to befriend one's sexuality.

Befriending One's Sexuality

The first step in the process of making friends with one's sexuality is to contact the repressed parts of oneself, and thereby reinitiate dialogue with one's body as well as with one's sexual feelings and desires. Such a search cannot be simply theoretical; it must be experiential as well. One needs to explore one's body to reawaken parts one has lost contact with. An important aid in that process is touching—learning to touch and be touched. When the University of Notre Dame began its germ-free laboratory, the staff members were quite dismayed to discover that the first rats were dying of genital-urinary and gastrointestinal disorders. They had the best diet and an ideal living situation. A young woman who had worked in a zoo told the staff that the rats needed to be touched. Thereafter, the staff would touch the rats every day, and they lived.[17] Likewise, in humans, touching is an important factor in emotional growth and in the capacity for intimacy. For example, babies who do not receive sufficient tactile stimulation—hugging, cuddling, kissing—do not develop normally. In the first months after birth, touching can mean the difference between life and death. In my clinical practice, I frequently find priests and religious using sex as a means of getting tactile stimulation. What many really want is to be held in close physical contact. Similarly, I often find in disturbed marriages that the spouses who are starved for tactile stimulation tend to limit the expression of that need to sexual contact. Sex serves only one function of touching, however, and probably not the most important. Nonsexual tactile stimulation is important for

---

17. Ashley Montague, *Touching* (New York: Harper and Row, 1978).

both men and women throughout their lives. There are many natural opportunities to learn to experience tactile stimulation. Washing and combing one's hair, taking a shower, and drying oneself are such opportunities, if done slowly and with awareness of one's feelings. Giving and receiving massages and giving a massage to oneself are also good ways to contact one's body.[18]

For those with rigid bodies and tense muscles, various types of body and movement therapies can be helpful. Rolfing, bioenergetics, Reichian therapy, Feldenkrais, and dance and movement therapies are some examples. Nonverbal therapies such as Gestalt, psychodrama, and music can also be useful approaches, in addition to fantasy and dreams.

To the degree that chronic tension immobilizes our bodies, our capacity for pleasure is reduced. We experience pleasure when we totally involve ourselves in an activity—with mind, body, feelings, and spirit. To reclaim our bodies, pain needs to be replaced by pleasure, and despair by positive feelings. The way to pleasure is through the pain, and the path to joy is through despair. Learning to release feelings of pain, sadness, and despair opens the way for positive feelings to flow into the body. Since holding our breath cuts off our feelings, learning to breathe deeply can evoke strong feelings and reawaken life in a deadened body.

Any emotion that cannot be released or transformed creates stress in the muscles. Emotions are charges of energy pressing for release. Thus sadness is released through crying. If crying is inhibited, then the muscles normally involved in crying become tense and restricted, particularly the muscles of the mouth, throat, chest, and abdomen. Every chronically tense muscle group represents an emotional conflict which is unresolved and probably repressed. Every chronically tense muscle also represents a negative attitude. Since it is blocking the expression of some impulse, it is in effect saying, "I won't."[19] Nonawareness and body rigidity are reinforced by rigid and negative attitudes

18. Zilbergeld, *Male Sexuality,* pp. 132-44.

19. Lowen, *Pleasure,* pp. 35-83.

and beliefs regarding the body and sexuality. Thus contacting one's body must also involve reeducation of the emotions and mental attitudes.

Awareness of one's body and especially its senses—sight, touch, smell, hearing, and fantasy—increases awareness of one's sexuality. Some studies suggest that men are sexually aroused by visual stimuli, whereas women are more responsive to tactile stimuli. Learning to use all our senses can enhance our capacity for sexual awareness. For example, there is a difference between seeing a sunset and experiencing a sunset. There is a difference between eating food and experiencing food. The next time you eat an apple, first touch it and explore its contour with your eyes closed. When you cut it open, listen to it and smell it. Fantasize yourself as the apple, and what it is like to have someone bite into you. Imagine the apple becoming part of your body. Taste its various flavors. In doing exercises like this, eating becomes a wholly different experience. The main reason why people become overweight is that they have lost touch with their bodies and no longer can listen to them. They do not know if they are hungry or not. They have lost touch with the body's natural wisdom.

Experiencing Sexuality

Sexual awareness is primarily the ability to name a sexual feeling or desire and allow it into consciousness. It is not enough to label one's sexual feelings and desires; one needs also to experience them. This means allowing oneself actually to feel sexual desire, needs, and arousal. Once an emotion arises, it tends to follow a natural course of its own—it is experienced, expressed in some form of bodily behavior, and discharged. However, every emotion does not need to be acted upon. Emotion and action are two distinct categories. What is required for one's well-being is that emotions be acknowledged and experienced. Once that is accomplished, then one can choose an appropriate response. Emotions in themselves are not always a suitable guide for behavior. Behavioral expression depends on many factors such as values, one's situation, perceived consequences, and the inherent meaning of the fact. Thus to think about something, to fantasize, to feel, and to act are all distinct processes. To equate them is magical thinking. To think about sex is not the same as doing it.

To facilitate the experience of emotions, it is helpful to learn to focus on them. Focusing means learning to sit with emotions without judgment or analysis. One simply pays attention to them. For those who tend to somatize their feelings, the first step is to listen to body symptoms and enter into dialogue with them. Give the symptom an image by attributing shape, color, and size to it. Thus if you have a headache, become the headache and let the headache tell you what it is trying to express.

Acceptance of Sexuality

Once we have acknowledged and experienced our sexuality, we are able to repossess that part of ourselves and integrate it into our total personality. Ownership of one's sexuality is the basis of self-acceptance. Acceptance demands we experience our sexuality without censorship or interfering self-criticism. Feelings are neutral, including sexual ones.

Sexual Communication and Expression

In the process of contacting and befriending one's sexuality, a gradual awakening occurs which probably will display all the characteristics described earlier as indicative of immature psychosexual intimacy. Repression has built up a volcano which may now erupt into a constant obsession with sex and a compulsive urge to discharge tension. Beginning attempts to explore intimate relationships may be clinging, possessive, and indiscriminate in their choice of object. Intimacy needs may be sexualized and acted out as such.

Repression is like frostbite. Once it begins to thaw, numbness gives way to pain. Thus, in the process of emerging sexual awareness, fear, rage, pain, and sadness may begin to surface.

Infatuation and falling in love are often the initial stages of growth in intimacy. As in the case of sexuality in general, awareness and compassionate acceptance are the key to a healthy integration of infatuation. It is difficult when infatuated to distin-

guish sexual feelings and needs from genital urgency. Nonjudgmental and nonmoralistic guidance can help to facilitate that
distinction. Infatuated people feel an urgent need for warmth,
comfort, and security. As the illusion of their romantic yearnings is purified by the fire of reality, they tend to become disillusioned and are left feeling cold, frightened, and alone.[20] Two
values can assist growth through this process. First, abstinence
as a value can help one to explore the deeper meaning of sexual
urges. For example, during a fast an overeater may realize that
the desire for food is not based on physical hunger but on a need
for affection. Likewise, sexual fasting allows deeper unmet
needs to become part of the inner dialogue.

Second, solitude and prayer are important, especially for the
celibate. Through solitude and silence, we are able to transform
our loneliness into hospitality. In solitude, we come to realize
that an unhappy loneliness reflects our inner poverty. An immature person expects others to fulfill his or her needs. It is
through solitude we discover our own inner richness. Deprivation becomes an opportunity for insight and growth.

Often infatuated people are not ready for insight. Their
urgent grasping for gratification must loosen and die before
insight can occur.[21]

In solitude we learn to pray out of our condition. In doing so,
we begin to bring to God our sexual struggle and to talk to him
about it. Instead of fighting distractions, the distractions become part of a prayerful dialogue.

The more we are able to experience a mature psychosexual
celibacy, the more we will be able to make a mature commitment
to celibacy. If we are not free to express our sexuality, then we
are not free to choose celibacy. Celibacy is a continuous process
of becoming. To be totally celibate is to be totally sexual, even if
unexpressed genitally. When we read the great mystics like John
of the Cross or Teresa of Avila or the writer of the Song of

---

20. Tyrrell, *Urgent Longings,* p. 86.

21. Ibid.

Songs, we are impressed by how sensual and full of sexual imagery the language is. Mystical experiences and sexual orgasm have a lot in common. Both are examples of self-surrender of the self-consciousness of the ego. Sexual orgasm expresses through a biological experience the deeper experience of humanity's unity with nature and the universe. The goal of celibacy is likewise a self-surrender—a letting go of human consciousness and boundaries with the resultant emergence of a deeper union with self, with our fellow men and women, and with our God.

Both the celibate and the genitally active person strive to attain this union, and in the process both may draw on the power of meditation, solitude, mysticism, and self-awareness. Thus the ultimate goal of the celibate and the sexual person is the same. For the celibate it is union with God, and through God with all people and creation. For the sexual person, it is physical union with people, and through that union, union with God and all his creation.

Homosexuality: A Special Issue in Psychosexual Maturity

All of the above discussion is relevant to both hetereosexuals and homosexuals. However, societal reactions and labeling present special challenges to the process of psychosexual maturation for the homosexual.

Homosexual Identity

Sexual awakening is a confusing process for most. However, society and family provide role models and definitions to facilitate sexual awareness and sexual identity. For homosexuals, there are no role models. Every other minority group has a place where its members can be affirmed in their identity. Blacks, for example, even if not acknowledged or affirmed by the larger society, can be black at home and so defined. Homosexuals usually have nowhere to turn for help to clarify their sexual emergence—to tell them who or what they are. When they begin to discover their same-sex orientation, they usually do not greet it with joy. Even before they discover their unique sexual identity, they know that society considers homosexuality a negative value. Religion labels homosexuals as immoral; society as illegal; and medicine as ill. Even though these labels have been modified recently, the stigma remains. Thus homosexuals are encouraged to deny their sexuality and fragment themselves into an appearance of normality. They begin to live in two worlds—one inside their minds and feelings, and one that they share with others. They feel pressure to enclose their sexuality in a private prison to preserve it from external threats and judgments. The effects of this double life are feelings of fear, guilt, anger, and confusion. At the same time homosexuals feel estranged from and distrustful of their own families and friends.

When someone says, "I don't know who I am," he or she is in effect saying, "I don't know what I feel, what I want, or what I need."[22] Because of societal reactions and labels, homosexuals are encouraged to deny and repress homosexual feelings, needs, and desires. Consequently, they feel inner confusion and doubts, or are simply unaware of their sexual identity. Thus they may look outside of themselves for positive meaning and affirmation, and try to fulfill societal expectations and images. Since these images tend to be heterosexual, the homosexual "will subvert his body and manipulate the environment to maintain that image. He will adapt a role based on this image, and will equate his identity with this role."[23] Homosexuals may enter into hetereosexual marriages, while denying their homosexual orientation.

Initially, a child does not have an identity, but a collection of identifications. She or he identifies with significant adults at first, and later with peers. Eventually out of this network of

22. Alexander Lowen, *The Betrayal of the Body* (New York: Collier Books, 1967), p. 232.

23. Ibid., p. 233.

identifications, the child must synthesize a unique self and identity.[24] An important aspect of that process of synthesis is a sense of our uninterrupted history. To be able to achieve this sense of connection with our past, we need others who have shared our history, and who can affirm our continuity.[25] As Erik Erikson argues, "A healthy individual is one that is open to change and redefinition but above all is rooted in an historical, traceable past, so that through all there runs an invigorating sense of sameness"—what William Kilpatrick calls "continuity."[26] In his discussion of Erikson, Kilpatrick continues: "It is imperative that our sense of identity be reinforced by significant others."[27]

One of the central issues for homosexuals is a lack of such continuity. Who are the significant others for homosexuals when their sexual awakening emerges? Rarely do they know someone else who is homosexual. Once they begin to realize their unique identity they need to distance themselves from significant others with whom they had previously identified, as well as from those institutions that have labeled them negatively. If homosexuals are to explore their unique identity, they need the support of other homosexuals with whom they can identify. Obtaining this reinforcement usually entails "coming out," not only to themselves but also to other homosexuals.

Coming Out

The purpose of coming out is to help homosexuals believe in and accept the rightness of their own sexual identity, and to foster self-respect. Coming out means to acknowledge, experience, and accept their homosexual feelings and attractions. Since identity is achieved through identification with others, it may also be important for them to find a homosexual support

---

24. William Kilpatrick, *Identity and Intimacy* (New York: Dell, 1975), pp. 23-4.

25. Ibid., p. 4.

26. Ibid., p. 29.

27. Ibid., p. 30.

group that can affirm and help clarify their identity. Heterosexuals usually come out out at puberty, whereas homosexuals often do so later—usually during their twenties or thirties. Consequently, one might expect emerging homosexuals to manifest behavior similar to that exhibited by heterosexuals in their teens. Coming out for the celibate often is a clandestine and underground experience since most religious communities and dioceses seem not to tolerate such a public identity. Such a rule, often combined with homophobia, encourages either repression with all its consequences or a secret life outside the convent, rectory, or religious community.

The "coming out" process is similar to the stages described by Elizabeth Kübler-Ross in *Death and Dying*.[28] First there is denial. In the first stage, many homosexuals will do everything to prove that they are not homosexual. Also, they tend to be homophobic. They can tell the loudest antihomosexual jokes and be the most critical of other homosexuals. Thus those people who feel strongly negative toward homosexuals may actually be defending against their own unconscious homosexual desires. During the second stage, anger, homosexuals begin to react to the rejections and hurts and judgments of the past. Their anger and sometimes rage will often lead them to disown those institutions that symbolize rejection such as religion, law enforcement, and mental health. The third stage is characterized by reconciliation with their homosexual identity. Their anger becomes tempered with compassion. The final stage is acceptance. They now begin to look upon their homosexual orientation as a gift and a positive reality. They may realize, for example, that the male homosexual can teach others that women are people, not sexual objects. Heterosexual women are often attracted to homosexual men because such men respect their womanhood and are often in touch with their own femininity. Likewise, homosexuals can be a gift to same-sex persons by not being afraid to express physical affection and warmth to them.

---

28. Elizabeth Kübler-Ross, *On Death and Dying* (New York: Macmillan, 1971).

The achievement of a stable identity, which includes sexual identity, is a prerequisite for the capacity for intimate relationships. To facilitate that process, homosexuals need to be affirmed and accepted for who they are. This often may require seeking out a support system that includes some other homosexuals who are secure in their identity. Organizations like Dignity in the Catholic Church are good examples of such support systems.

I once asked a lesbian what the most difficult experience was that she had encountered in accepting her homosexuality. She said, "When I fell in love the first time with another woman, I couldn't share it with anyone. I couldn't tell my family or friends. That was very painful."

Homosexuals who engage in secret passages and try to appear heterosexual risk division of their inner identity, and thus prolong the achievement of personality and psychosexual integration.

Role of Religious Community in Psychosexual Maturity

In concluding this discussion of growth in psychosexual intimacy, I will consider the ways in which religious communities both aid and hinder the psychosexual maturity and intimacy of their members. By religious communities I mean all communities in which people officially dedicated to religious ministry live and work. Thus I am including convents, rectories, religious houses, and in general any group that serves as a significant support system for a priest, brother, sister, or lay minister.

Work Versus Community Orientation

One of the great hindrances to intimacy is a community whose primary orientation is work. In such a context, celibacy tends to be defined as functional, as enabling its members to become better workers. The popular notion is that it frees one to be more available as a minister.

When work is the main orientation, everything is scheduled to meet the needs of the job. One's personal needs and the needs of the community are secondary. Often there is little separation between residence and work. Even when there is physical distance, an analysis of conversations in the residence suggests there is little psychological separation. In addition, in such communities, some members are frequently moved, making it very difficult to establish sustaining and intimate relationships.[29]

Although communities are not substitute parents and need not attempt to satisfy all the needs of their members, they are called to be witnesses of God's all-embracing love. Community is not a given; it needs to be created.

Community as Facilitator of Intimate Relationships

If the religious system is to facilitate intimacy and build community, it needs to provide an accepting, nonjudgmental atmosphere in which developmental needs can be explored and struggled with. This first condition assumes that the community provides time and space for its members to be together. Second, it presupposes an atmosphere conducive to open, direct, and honest communication. Such a model would suggest that members talk about their relationships with one another. In that context, anger, jealousy, fear, and other emotions are honestly shared without recrimination. Thus, for example, if a particular exclusive friendship has developed which seems inimical to community, the couple in question would feel free to discuss their relationship openly. By so doing, they are relating it to the community. Then the community becomes the context in which to negotiate relationships and work out their meaning in the context of other significant relationships and personal commitments to the community. At the same time, the discussion affords the opportunity for community members to share their feelings of jealousy and unattractiveness, which often underlie criticism of particular friendships.

In such a community atmosphere, the homosexual would feel free to "come out" to his or her community and still be ac-

---

29. William R. Coulsen, *A Sense of Community* (Columbus, Ohio: Charles E. Merrill, 1973), pp. 138-47.

cepted, without risk of job discrimination in the future. My impression is that gay clergy and religious who have come out are frequently excluded from positions on formation staffs and in administration. Achieving such an open community may demand the services of an outside facilitator with professional expertise.

Role of the Superior or Director

Superiors or directors of religious communities set the tone. If they want to foster mature psychosexual intimacy among community members, they need first to become comfortable and accepting of their own sexuality, whether it be homosexual or heterosexual. A repressed superior will not be able to tolerate an open, nonjudgmental experimental environment, which is a prerequisite for growth. Repressed people in authority tend to promote a community atmosphere that is sterile and destructive. If superiors see themselves primarily as guardians of rules, then the community will be efficient but will probably lack real warmth. For intimacy to grow, there needs to be an element of unguardedness. Intimacy is a mystery. One cannot predict its outcome. One must trust its process and be open to it. Thus the community needs to have a sense of process and growth and development, and to embody this understanding in its rules and formation.

Although I have no statistics to substantiate it, my impression is that homosexuals are more present among clergy and religious than in the general population. One of the greatest obstacles to intimacy is a homophobic atmosphere. Reeducation and openness to homosexuals in the community is part of the resolution.

Last, and most important, the community needs to provide an atmosphere conducive to solitude and prayer. Prayer and intimate friendships are two pillars of support for celibates. At the same time, celibacy is an expression of mature psychosexual intimacy with oneself, with one's neighbor, and with one's God. The absence of a prayer life and of close intimate friends may mean that one is not living a true celibate commitment but rather a sterile, lifeless abstinence, which hinders God's life both in oneself and in the expression of one's ministry.

Gong Shu, M.A., A.T.R., is a full-time art therapist at the House of Affirmation in Webster Groves, Missouri. Born and raised in China, Ms. Gong holds a bachelor's degree in foreign languages, pursued graduate studies at Yale University and the University of California at Berkeley, and was awarded master's degrees in comparative literature and art therapy. She holds a certificate from St. Louis Gestalt Institute as a trained Gestalt therapist. Ms. Gong has taught painting, art history, literature, and oriental philosophy at various colleges and universities including Saint Louis University, Washington University, and Webster College. She has conducted many workshops and classes on Taoism and Chinese painting. Her paintings are included in private collections in China and the United States.

Creative Relating

Gong Shu

Creativity is a spontaneous expression of the vitality of life. It is marked by innocence, freshness, uniqueness, unadorned devotion, and full concentration of the self in the process. It is an assertion of one's being in the world—like grass sprouting on the ground, a fawn leaping in the wood, a dolphin frolicking in the ocean, or a child rolling on a sandy beach. It is marked by excitement, authenticity, joy, and total involvement of the self—in the world, not in detachment or alienation.

One day, some time ago, I left my youngest daughter, Mei-ling, at her kindergarten. As I was walking away I saw Chris, a boy her age, run toward her. The two of them embraced and then held hands and walked to a sandbox to play. Such spontaneity, such total involvement of the self in the immediate situation, such innocence, freshness, and excitement is what I mean by creativity. There is a genuine meeting of the essential selves, without masks, without calculation. This is creative relating. Children know it well.

Creative Process

In discussing creativity, I am confining myself to the process. The creative process *is* relating. One does not create in a vacuum, whether this process involves art materials, music, science, or another person. Creativity is *relating* and it is also a way of living. Creative relating is characterized by *openness*—openness to the always new, always changing environment or to the other. It involves mutuality—the self provides an environment for the other, in which the potentials of the other can be realized. This in turn enhances and actualizes the potentialities of the self. All genuine creative growth involves a spontaneous interplay of complementary forces and a production of something new, a synthesizing or harmonizing of previously distinct components. It also means acceptance and affirmation of the always new, unique moment and phenomenon.

Ideas such as these are found in many religious as well as many humanistic thinkers—in Erich Fromm, Carl Jung, Abraham Maslow, Carl Rogers, Martin Buber, Gabriel Marcel, Paul Tillich, Rollo May, and others. They are also found in ancient Taoism, which is my own native philosophy. I would like to share with you a brief account of how Taoism sees creative relating.

Let me start with a statement from a Taoist philosopher, Lao Tzu, regarding creativity:

> All things originate in *Tao*.
> They are nurtured by *Te,*
> Becoming things, they gain forms
> Through their innate tendencies [*Shih*]
>   they become complete.
>
> All things originate in *Tao*
> By *Te* they are nourished,
> Guided, cared for,
> Sheltered, comforted,
> Developed, and protected.
> Creating without taking credit,
> Nourishing without interfering.
> This is the nature of *Te*. [1]

Here *Tao* simply means the way—the way life is, the way things are. Tao is the spontaneous expression of life itself. Thus,

---

1. Lao Tzu, *Tao Te Ching,* chap. 51, ed. Wang P'i in *Ssu Pu Pei Yao,* vol. 341, compiled by Ting P'u Tzu et al. (Taipei: Chung Hua Press, 1965-66), pp. 9-10, translation my own.

Tao finds expression in everything. *Te* means potentials, the creative energy within each of us. Lao Tzu's statement about Te implies that every organism has an innate potential and an innate tendency to sustain, enhance, and complete itself. An organism inherently functions to find harmonious relationships with its environment that suit its needs, potentials, and resources. The innate tendency works through the receptivity and responding behavior of the organism within its environment. Through this living process the organism will actualize its potentials as best it can. This is the organism's spontaneous, natural growth process. Lao Tzu expressed this insight in chapter twenty-five of *Tao Te Ching*:

> Man's standard is Earth.
> Earth's standard is Heaven.
> Heaven's standard is *Tao*.
> *Tao's* standard is the spontaneous.[2]

Separation and Differentiation

To be creative, then, is to follow one's spontaneous growth process. This process of growth is expressed in the interaction of opposites, the *yin* and the *yang*. Yin and yang refers to the play of opposites, each of which influences the other. This mutuality is interdependence: the opposites mutually depend on each other to be what they are. Even more, they are present to some degree in each other. This is the basis of what Taoists call *interpenetration and the great sympathy.* This is the Taoist way of pointing out our capacity to be deeply touched by and in tune with, say, suffering people across the world, with surprises of nature, or with each other when we first meet.

This play of opposites and interdependence can be observed in nearly every organism. It is seen as sexual in nature, in the sense that life works through pairs of opposites which unite together to foster new life and growth. In sexual opposites some degree of each opposite is concealed in the other—some degree of

2. Lao Tzu, *Tao Te Ching,* chap. 25, quoted in Fung Yu-Lan, *A History of Chinese Philosophy,* vol. 1 (Princeton, N.J.: Princeton University Press, 1952), p. 187.

feminine in the masculine, or the masculine in the feminine. Jung recognized this, as does Taosim and the philosophy of yin-yang polarity; this sharing is the basis of organic growth and creativity, and thus of human creativity as well. Opposites seek each other out in a relating of love. Love, the urge for unity, is the generative center of creativity and relationship. Interestingly, this profound thought is also expressed by Socrates in his speech on love, in Plato's *Symposium*.

This creative urge for relating and for unity is the source of all energies of life. Dylan Thomas speaks of the creative urge in this way:

> The force that through the green fuse drives the flower
> Drives my green age; . . .
> The Force that drives the water through the rocks
> Drives my red blood.[3]

Separation and differentiation are also inevitable stages of the creative process.

Encounter and Relationship

From separation and differentiation one moves to encounter and relationship. It is *Eros,* the yearning for union, that urges one to reach out, to create. This desire for reaching out can be transmuted into a universal love, *agape,* which enables us to unite and reach harmony with all of life. Creativity requires one to accept change and separation. Creativity requires one to let go; a child must let go of the mother, a mother must let go of the child. This detachment requires each to have the courage to flow with the moment and accept change and difference, to accept each moment as a unique phenomenon. Creative relating is a process of interdependence within which each person must accept himself or herself as a unique being.

Harmony is created out of diversity, not out of identity. In the creative process of relating one loses the self in the unity; one is changed, yet remains completely in touch with the self as an individual. One needs to be completely aware of the uniqueness

3. Dylan Thomas, "The Force that through the Green Fuse," *Collected Poems* (New York: New Directions Books, 1953), p. 10.

of the individual and have the courage to be fully present as the real self even in time of stress and doubt, for creativity is the dynamic interplay of opposite forces.

To be fully creative is to be fully *present,* to be fully involved in the moment. Creativity is a person's total involvement in an expression of his or her being. It is like the dancer who creates the phenomenon of dance. The dance exists only insofar as the dancer is in the process of creating it. The poet W. B. Yeats said it this way:

O chestnut-tree, great-rooted blossomer,
Are you the leaf, the blossom or the bole?
O body swayed to music, O brightening glance,
How can we know the dancer from the dance?[4]

The dancer and the dance are one.

The dancer is concentrating on the process of dancing and is fully aware of the total phenomenon of dance. But if the dancer becomes conscious of herself as making the dance, the dance breaks. If she is conscious of her balance, she loses it. The student driver who is learning to drive a stick-shift car is a similar example; the minute he tries to memorize the gear-shifting process, the car stalls. If a chef is worried about her sick husband at home, she burns the food.

Genuine creativity, then, requires full concentration and full awareness—there is no division between the creator and the created. Genuine creativity is a total immersion of the self in the process.

As Yeats's words express, the creative person is in intimate touch with the creative process, so intimate that the dancer and the dance are indistinguishable. The Zen teacher D. T. Suzuki said regarding this state of creativity, "When a man reaches this stage of 'spiritual' development, he is a Zen artist of life. He does not need, like the painter, a canvas, brushes, and paints. . . . His hands and feet are the brushes and the whole universe

---

4. W. B. Yeats, "Among School Children," *Collected Poems of W. B. Yeats* (New York: Macmillan, 1952), p. 214.

is the canvas on which he depicts his life. . . . This picture is history."[5]

Artist of Life

What does all this mean for relationships? In creating dance, the dancer becomes one with the dance. In living creatively, the individual is an artist of life—the person, the process, and the work of art are one. Creativity is spontaneous, total absorption and involvement in whatever is present. In creative relating, the individuals are fully involved, fully present, and aware of their full being, their mutuality. The person and the process are one. When this happens, an hour, two hours, a day spent with another or others is exhilarating. Remember how one's spirit can be lifted and energized by an affirming glance from a total stranger in a subway crowd? In this fleeting moment one experiences the other's unbroken spontaneous presence and responsiveness.

In the creative process of relating, a person is fully immersed in an experience to the extent that he or she is lost as a separate being, yet remains uniquely free as an individual. The person experiences for the first time with full awareness the unique reality of the moment.

This ideal relationship with the world is "pure experience." To be in "pure experience" requires one to see the world without "desire," without expectation, without attachment, without addictions. All of life is nurtured by universal forces which bring out the potential of each organism. The Taoist calls this the infinite ground of sympathy. Intimacy grows out of the self's genuine relatedness with the world and with others—the total immersion of the self in the experience. This immersion gives meaning to life. Intimacy is full relatedness—the feeling of connection and the feeling of being in touch. This genuine relatedness is what I call creative relating.

However, given the social and economic conditions of today, this creative relating is difficult to achieve. The daily news is

---

5. In D. T. Suzuki's foreword to Eugen Herrigel's *Zen in the Art of Archery* (New York: McGraw-Hill, 1964), p. 15.

filled with sad and terrible events. We need constant renewal in the face of so many forces that threaten our creative relating.

Obstacles to Creative Relating

Let me point out now some of the obstacles to creative relating and give some examples. Let us also remember that these obstacles in our experience are the artist's materials we are challenged to transform into creative relating.

This time is very challenging. The current culture reveals a highly developed "left-brain" orientation. It values linear, verbal, and analytical thinking, and leaves little room for, or sensitivity to, "right-brain" activity, that is, intuitive awareness which sees the gestalt, the whole configuration. Right-brain activity can be cultivated only through sensory and intuitive awareness. Recognizing this state of affairs, we must allow intuition to guide us and allow our senses to experience the world in order to absorb and participate in its richness.

In this highly developed technocratic or "left-brain" society, intellect and even so-called spiritual growth have outstripped emotional development. Bodily functions of sensing, feeling, tasting, even seeing or hearing, are at times inhibited or repressed by the intellect. A person eventually becomes a total thinking being, a functionary, devoid of feeling and of full spontaneous, intuitive awareness of what he or she is experiencing. The consequence of such repression of emotional experience is "meaninglessness," "emptiness." The joy of life is missing.

Many writers have expressed concern about how our way of life constricts our experience. Fromm noted the way in which everyone is conscious of using everyone else.[6] People become commodities. Recently, just as the professional football strike was starting, the owner of one of the teams was giving the players a pep talk about how great and important all of them were. Then he made a slip. He said, enthusiastically, "You are

---

6. Erich Fromm, *The Sane Society* (New York: Holt, Rinehart, and Winston, 1960), p. 139.

our commodities." One player asked another, "What is a commodity?" Then he understood what he meant to the owner: he was a thing to be bought, sold, and controlled, an object of investment and exploitation.

Marcel, too, distinguishes between being and having.[7] Being is who a person is, his or her real self, living in a world of persons and creativity. Having is related to functions; a function, or we may say, a role, is something one *has,* not something one *is* at bottom. The function lives in a world of things.

Buddhism also distinguishes between *being* and being *this* or *that.* We run serious risks of identifying ourselves simply with being this or that—a function, a role, an identity. In doing so, we lose our creative selves and freedom, and reduce ourselves to the limitations imposed by social roles.

Consider how such a reduction of ourselves hinders creative relating. Our relationships, whether with people, nature, or things, can be blocked by various fixations, or attachments, whether these attachments are to past, to future, to a person, to an idea, or to values set up by others. Separation of the self and the experience will result if our minds are bound by such fixations.

If we rely on *past* experience, we are dealing with a concept of the situation rather than the situation itself. We lack awareness of the actual present circumstances. Similarly, when we obsessively anticipate and prepare for the future, we are less aware than we need to be of what is going on at the present. Attachments to the past or to the future deter us from immediate contact with the present, its "hereness" and "nowness." We become outsiders in regard to what is immediately present to us. Our energy is locked up in various other temporal/spatial dimensions to a degree that we are not able to participate or function fully in the present. We lose awareness of our own immediate needs. By doing this we become alienated from the *real self,* as Karen Horney calls it. We become outsiders to our own experience, detached and disengaged from our actual awareness

---

7. Gabriel Marcel, *Being and Having* (New York: Harper and Row, 1965), p. 150.

of the present. In this state of alienation and disengagement intimacy is impossible.

We may also become fixated on values set up by the environment—the "shoulds" and "should nots," the standards of others. We become ever watchful and judgmental of our own behavior. We use the values of others to modify our natural responses, in order to win their approval. I myself often feel this kind of conflict when I am asked to do paintings for commission, in contrast to how I feel when I paint spontaneously, for myself. The judgmental attitude always separates the self from the act. It causes a conflict between the *real self* and the image of the self. In this experience the "I" is constantly examining something in order to change it, so there is always a dualistic conflict and therefore a protracted separation. As Horney says:

> As soon as . . . [the individual who needs] to be liked by everybody becomes compulsive, the genuineness of his feeling diminishes . . . [and] his spontaneous interest in work itself decreases. Conflicting compulsive drives . . . impair his integration, his faculty to decide and give direction. . . . neurotic pseudo-solutions though representing attempts at integration, . . . deprive him of autonomy because they become a compulsive way of living.[8]

This compulsiveness involves repetition of expectations, and can lead to self-torture. For example, a client of mine was so obsessed with the fear of rejection, and fear of not being liked, that she withdrew from involvement in group art therapy. She usually sat in a corner, feeling angry at herself and the therapist, because, as she said, "I don't know how to draw. No matter what I do, it will be wrong. I can't please you." Today, following her therapy, this person is back in her community, able to relate more creatively and self-confidently.

If we single out some dimensions or parts of ourselves either to avoid or pursue obsessively, we create energy problems. Our energy becomes locked in self-condemnation, fear, and compulsive striving. Experiencing only parts of ourselves makes us

---

8. Karen Horney, *Neurosis and Human Growth* (New York: W. W. Norton, 1950), p. 179.

see ourselves in a piecemeal way, as if we were merely the sum total of disconnected parts. "This is known in psychiatric literature as *compartmentalization* or *psychic fragmentation.* . . . [the person] has no feeling for himself as a whole organism."[9]

When certain emotions are suppressed or concentrated on exclusively and compulsively, natural relationships are inhibited or curtailed. Rogers contrasts the closed and the open state in these terms:

> To the extent that the individual is denying to awareness (or repressing, if you prefer that term) large areas of his experience, then his creative formings may be pathological or socially evil, or both. To the degree that the individual is open to all aspects of his experience, and has available to his *awareness* all the varied sensings and perceivings which are going on within his organism then the novel products of his interaction with his environment will tend to be constructive both for himself and other.[10]

There are serious consequences when full awareness of ourselves and the other is blocked. Full awareness requires great continuous energy, for it is easy to slip out of such concentrated involvement. We may feel bored and alienated, like an outsider to our experience. Nothing is new; everything is the same. "I've heard it all," is the lament. When we have that attitude, natural responses are deadened. We are not alert to the nuances of the moment, to the spontaneous response. We are bored because we think everything we are experiencing is the same old thing, identical to what we have already encountered. Life becomes meaningless, empty.

What is happening here? Look carefully at how the mind works when we are bored—a potentially rich experience is reduced to a repeatable concept, to a category. In this state, what

---

9. Ibid.

10. Carl Rogers, "Toward a Theory of Creativity," in *Creativity and Its Cultivation,* ed. H. H. Anderson (New York: Harper and Row, 1959), pp. 73-74.

is encountered is a concept, an idea of a person or an event, not the actual person or event confronted. A concept acquired from the past surfaces to judge and to analyze the present. As a result the full present, with all its subtle nuances, multiple dimensions, and fascinating mystery is lost. "He is a German: he can't express his feelings." "He is just an intellectual." "She is an artist, an irrational person." "They are Arabs; you can't understand them." "I'm depressed. Nothing ever changes; I feel hopeless."

All these expressions show the mind reducing the profound subtlety and nuances of the moment to repetitive ideas, to abstractions, to fixations. No creative relating is possible when we are locked into such abstractions, fixations, and expectations. Boredom results.

Honesty is also essential to creative relating. When feelings are not directly and honestly expressed, we deny ourselves. In the process relationship is stifled, and growth in relationship and in the self is impeded. This result is especially evident when dealing with feelings generally considered negative, for example, anger. In the impulse to repress the surge of anger all feelings are repressed. A habit of suppressing anger may lead to passive-aggressive behavior, or to self-torturing or somatic symptoms, such as headaches, upset stomachs, or more lasting chronic debilities.

Emotions—even negative ones—released in creative relationships, centered in loving and caring, produce a generative power that is mutually shared and mutually energizing, rising above the petty pain of "hurt feelings." What happens here is that energy customarily used to block the expression of anger (or other emotions) is turned to creative purpose.

Thus, by not expressing feelings directly and honestly, we become alientated from ourselves. In such states of alienation, genuine intimacy is impossible.

The solution is to let go of habitual clingings, let go of the old scripts of the past, let go of anticipation of the future. The individual can then flow spontaneously on the great waves of nature without fear, as T'ao Yuan-ming, the Chinese poet, said. Life requires a great deal of risk taking; in this risk taking each moment is lived new and fresh, and experience is magnified. When one plunges fully into the constant process of change, one experiences life intensely and achieves an intimate harmony with all of life.

The following is a personal example of creative relating. My nine-year-old daughter knows how to get her needs met. Waiting for me to embrace her, and becoming disappointed when I am distracted by someone or something else, she does not pout or go off alone to sulk. Instead she will come to me and say, "Mama, cuddle," or "Mama, I want you to spend more time with me." Obviously, I am not able to spend as much time with her as she needs. But she does not hesitate to express her feelings, and we usually work out something so she will not feel neglected. Children know how to be spontaneous and honest. They may be our best teachers.

But being honest does not mean to descend to carping criticism or to flay the other with self-righteousness, with distorted personal, or rather, egoistic claims. This is false honesty, honesty that is no more than a mask for sadistic oppression. Authentic honest expression of emotion deepens a relationship and makes creative relating possible.

Creativity and Environment

To be creative is to free oneself for total involvement in an existential moment—body, mind, and spirit. The first step is to cultivate the ability to integrate the "right-brain" functioning with the "left-brain" functioning that our world demands. This freedom to feel, to sense, to emote, to experience the world with our bodies as well as our minds, requires a return to intuitive knowing. We must learn from the child and bring the child's innocence, open honesty, curiosity, enthusiasm, and excitement into everyday living. It means slowing down, escaping the "push-button" culture syndrome—instant breakfast, instant gratification. We must take time to *experience* life's phenomena. Most of us live in a "hothouse," in air-conditioned cars, air-conditioned rooms cut off from nature in all its multifold dimensions. Creativity lies in touching, feeling the natural environment.

Relating to the environment and relating to other persons go together. Creative relating is a meeting of real persons who are genuinely caring and honestly free and open to each other. It is a spontaneous and effortless expression of each self toward the other.

Creative living demands trusting ourselves and owning all the dimensions of the self. It requires accepting the self as unique, whereby we can come to respect the uniqueness and dignity of the other.

In this creative process of relating we touch some thing within another and, freeing that person to develop his or her potential, in the meantime affirm the self. If change occurs in us or in the other, it is not through manipulation but through a spontaneous growth process of two persons genuinely relating.

Genuine relating is a sharing of life and life's experiences, fully, freely, and honestly, *without* risk of loss of identity or of trespass of our own boundaries.

Genuine relating involves the whole person in the creative process. This process emerges within vital experience in the flow of real feelings, in our intimate relating to nature, to ourselves, and to others.

To be creative is to encounter the world with our *real self,* with all of our dimensions, our own convictions and values, not with the "shoulds" and "should nots" that are the standards of others. Creativity is the process that actualizes our potentials as humans. To be creative makes us whole.

We can see, then, the profound mystery of creative relating. It involves nothing less than our whole self, in every moment of existence/being. It demands total absorption in the full scope of each present moment, with each person. To relate creatively is to be whole. To be whole is to be completely present in body, mind, and spirit, with each other and with our world in every encounter. In being whole we affirm all of life, and we can be more freely available to meet the needs and changes of each moment. We create each other, and share in creating the world.

Sister Kathleen E. Kelley, S.N.D., M.Ed., is director of the House of Affirmation in Webster Groves, Missouri. A member of the Boston Province of the Sisters of Notre Dame de Namur, Sr. Kelley received her undergraduate education at Emmanuel College in Boston and did graduate work in counseling at Boston College. Before joining the staff of the House of Affirmation, she served on her province administration team and held the position of province personnel director. Sr. Kelley did career counseling at the House of Affirmation in Whitinsville before her appointment as director of the Webster Groves residential center. She has lectured extensively in the areas of mental health and the religious life in the United States and abroad.

To Be Full of Love

Kathleen E. Kelley

The topic of relationships definitely hit the commercial market in recent years. I fully expect to see a "Sale on Relationships" sign any day now. A glance through a bookstore will convince one that the self-help literature is the route to success if one will but face the "how to" issue: "how to win," "how to negotiate," "how to be one's own best friend." There are books on process, books on skills, and books on gaming, all offering the promise of a good or a better or perhaps the best relationship possible. There is a decided emphasis on intimacy as the essential ingredient for health, with a strong hint that one has missed life if one has not had the experience.

Advertising has relationships as a major focus. Things in relation to self form the strong bond between health and consumer. A "better you" or a "happier you" is promised if one would but buy this or that product. There is even slick marketing of relationship possibilities with God if one would but sign up for these meditation techniques or that course in spiritual success.

There is some bad news in all of this and some good news. The bad news is the sense that commercialism has made the experience of relationship into a packaged deal, similar to the fast-food experience; pay your money and get your product. The good news is the truth of what they are promoting. Advertisers pay a great deal of money to hit people where it hurts, and in this instance the area of relationships is the target.

There is a real and vital need for relationships in our lives. They are not merely nice additions to life, nor are they simply good for the memory banks of old age. Relationships are life's essential ingredients: the way that human beings find meaning in life and the way human beings place meaning on their endeavors.

Human life is simply defined by four fundamental relationships: to self; to God; to others; to one's world or environment. Commercialism touches the truth that relationships are central to life, but it minimizes the reality. Relationships are hard work and involve much more than process. They confront us with the tension inherent in the life of self versus the life with others; self-fulfillment versus self-sacrifice. On the human level relationships are essential for health; they are an ingredient for happiness and critical for growth.

> The interpersonal relationships into which the individual is born give him his first feelings toward himself. These early feelings for himself are the first form of his relationship to himself. They begin to set up a relation between the "I" and the "me." They give the first shape to his intrapsychic dynamics.
>
> As soon as the self is born, and constantly afterward to a greater or lesser degree, the self is in tension. This tension is a source of dynamic within the self, and in the relationships of the self to other selves, to the world, and to God. Tension in human beings may be thought of as the feeling that things are apart which belong together, and that they will draw still further apart unless something is done to relieve the tension. The tension may be felt as chiefly intrapsychic, or as chiefly interpersonal; but these two cannot be sharply separated, since intrapsychic tension tends to stimulate interpersonal tensions, and vice versa.[1]

On this same human level, we tend inward as beings filled with needs, personal concerns, and fears. This tension means a difficult balancing of the relationship between self and others.

---

1. Lewis Joseph Sherrill, *The Gift of Power* (New York: MacMillan, 1955), p. 165.

On the spiritual level, the call to service, to self-sacrifice, to holiness is through relationship. Paul's letter to the Ephesians suggests its importance for us: "God chose us in Him before the world began, to be holy and blameless in His sight, to be full of love" (Eph: 4-5). The Christian call, then, is to relationship, for love implies relationship.

Certainly, some of us can recall peak experiences in relationships, when we felt full of love; perhaps these times came in special moments of prayer, or in responding to a child or a needy person. For others, reading an article or seeing a news program may touch them in unexpected ways and draw them to greater involvement.

These peak experiences are special moments when our relatedness to one another is a felt and positive experience. However, they are peaks. Most of life deals with plateaus and valleys. It is in the "most of life" times—in the day-by-day living—that the demands of relationships are met and we are faced with our human selves trying to be full of love.

The Self

Faced with the challenge of growing through others, of growing in learning to love, we are confronted with the reality that, though we are called to be full of love, we are full of ourselves. In work, in relationships of service, in friendships, and in prayer, the self, with its needs, with its demands, with its insecurities and wants, keeps getting in the way. In reality we manage to inch into at least a tie for first place in our own attention. The challenge is how to become full of love, to move nearer to that, when in our honest moments we both realize and experience that we are so full of ourselves.

The past routes that have been traveled in dealing with this relational question have not proved too successful. The tension, the crux of growth and movement, was never acknowledged in this area of relationship and personal growth. Rather, one thought in either/or language and lived out of that mode of thinking. Either I was full of self and hence selfish or I was full of love and hence saintly. If the person acknowledged selfishness, the sure way to purge it from the self was self-denial and self-hatred, an encouragement to ignore and despise the self. If the person denied the self, then he or she was full of love and not human because there were no needs. In fact, there was no self—not a very compelling model of sainthood. The either/or mentality listened to only one half of the message; one was either human or holy.

And yet, life is not an either/or experience; it is a mixture. With regard to self/sainthood, sometimes self is at the center of the world, and sometimes the self is able to move aside for others. The most important realization in all of this is that one cannot move toward fulfilling the Christian call to be full of love without a self.

The self is the conduit for love. Through relationships, an individual moves along a continuum and back and forth along that continuum from being full of self to being full of love. Growth comes not by erasing or denying the self but by activating the self, by allowing relationships to transform the self. The task for the individual is to use the God-given human energy, the self, to transform that energy into love energy.

To respond to the call to be full of love is a great challenge in relationship. It means confronting the self/self-centeredness, needs, and insecurities, and choosing through that selfishness, those needs and fears, to make room for others; to put self aside for someone or something else. The opportunity for growth and movement toward fullness of love is available in every encounter of every day. The process for this kind of growth goes deeper than the "how to" books. It involves acknowledging the self with all its facets of humanness, bringing forth that self, sometimes needy, sometimes wounded, and then deciding who gets the center of attention. Sometimes the self has priority, sometimes others do. Going into relationship as a role, a stereotype, a "saint," does not lead one to fullness of love. It is buying into the consumer culture where robots are in vogue and relationships are programmed.

The responsible choice of this kind of difficult living centers around the individual's understanding and use of human energy.

Human Energy

Human energy is the stuff out of which love grows. Energy is the power for life and growth within the person, sparked by Divine Energy. We are made in the image of God and given power as cocreators of this world, with a mandate to care for the earth. On an individual level, this mandate instructs us to use our energy wisely.

The individual is presented with two choices. A person can use energy and let power flow through the self. If energy is used thoughtfully and responsibly, energy communicates life and recharges others and the self. Or a person can abuse energy, either by refusing to communicate it, whereupon it atrophies, or by dissipating it, whereupon it burns out. If an individual chooses to use energy, it is through the fundamental relationships that define life, where human self-centered energy becomes transformed into love energy. This transformation includes the self, since the self is the conduit of energy and hence of love.

The attention given to energy today suggests its importance to life. With regard to the human person, energy use is vital.

The focus on energy was highlighted these past months as the theme of the Knoxville World's Fair. The exhibits from around the world reminded us of some important realities: energy is power, sometimes used as a weapon, nation against nation; human beings have been wasteful and have forgotten that supplies are limited; costs are rising, and shortages are real. There is a plea for conservation and more creative use of energy. These same statements can be of import to human beings in their relationships.

Within individuals and between individuals, the use or abuse of energy/power builds up or tears down relationships. Energy—power in action—is a dynamic concept. We sometimes use the word when describing people: "the child is a bundle of energy"; "she burns off a lot of nervous energy"; "he complains of having no energy."

Within each person resides much potential energy. For it to be activated and promote growth and health for the person, it must have conduits, paths for it to get outside the individual. There are definite conduits within the person and definite signals within the person that energy needs to be released.

Energy is meant to flow through the total person. We speak of spiritual energy, intellectual energy, emotional and physical energy. The different aspects of the individual get charged and become powerful when energy flows through them. If persons allow energy to flow on all levels within them, they are experienced as "energetic," full of energy. This channeling of energy into the conduits of the person is hard work. There is a tendency to ignore certain aspects, resulting in blocked energy. Experience attests to this reality; for every energetic person, one who is power in action, there are two who are blocked in energy. We see people who are stressed—uptight—who in time burn out all their energy; others who are depressed, having pushed down their energy; others who seem scattered, without a focus, who end up dissipating their energy and feeling powerless. These people are not very successful in their relationships.

There are many ways that energy gets misused and hence relationships are thwarted. Fixation of energy is one way. All energy gets channeled into one aspect of the individual; either work or social causes, head or spirit. Relationship, particularly with the self, is fragmented. The only way the individual can relate is through the fixation. The fixation in one aspect suggests that the other areas of the person are being neglected.

Hoarding energy is another misuse. The individual keeps it all within the self, "spinnning his wheels" in preoccupation. Energy is spent going around in the circles of one's own mind. Worry, tension, obsessive thinking, and self-concern mark this kind of person. The dialogue within the self begins and ends with the word "I." "What am I going to do, eat, drink?" "Am I liked, loved, accepted, supported...?" Relationship is very difficult, if not impossible, because the person is too busy with self. Hopes of transforming this energy into love are slim.

Some individuals become energy-stompers. Whenever a feeling or need arises through which energy can flow, energy gets pushed down, down, down. Feelings are ignored. Anger in particular is denied. The person represses and eventually depresses the power. Like a muscle that has not been exercised, energy, and the human psyche, go limp. The person experiences being "energy-less." Relationships are too much because they depend on energy and the individual does not have any to give out.

There are other extremes concerning the use/misuse of energy that fall under the category of "high voltage"; for example, persons who are experienced as eternal energy-givers, leaving everyone around them exhausted. These people pour their energy outward, giving without limit or without awareness of their own needs. There is a sense that the human within them does not exist but has been given over to the control of unfocused energy. Relating with this type of person is like trying to connect with a tornado—one may be blown away with the energy.

These ways of using energy suggest wastefulness in that they do not move the individual toward others nor do they involve the person in the process of transformation.

Energy and Needs

For energy to be used responsibly it has to flow through the self. Energy has to have a conduit. The human conduit is a self, created with needs. Needs are signal systems that tell the individual where energy is lacking in the self. The most important use of energy within the human person is to give care to the self through listening to one's needs.

We all have spiritual, intellectual, physical, and emotional needs. When the system is in need of some attention and care, the need's signal system goes off, alerting the self that energy is required to pass through the conduit. Since it is energy, it goes out of the individual into relationship. To transform human energy into love energy, it has to go through the self. Energy is meant to bring life because it is power. Because it is dynamic, it is meant to flow through the conduits of the self.

Some people, however, equate paying attention to the needs of the self with absolute selfishness, and consequently they go to the opposite extreme of absolute denial of needs. Either extreme is a misuse of human power. Neither self-centeredness nor total denial of the self is a response to the call to human wholeness and holiness.

The arduous task of adult relationships is connected with how we choose to use our human energy to grow from being full of self to being full of love.

Human Wholeness

A human being is a complex creature with many facets and many needs. If a person learns to care for the self and develops all aspects of his or her being, such care will lead to wholeness. The choice is to allow energy to flow into all dimensions. If the individual pays attention to the self, the self becomes energized. If the self is ignored or denied, energy gets blocked and the person feels tense or depressed and drained, as if "somebody pulled the plug."

It is this self, with needs and with energy, that is brought into relationship with others. Relationships provide the experiences for transforming a person who is full of self to one full of love. Yet the self remains the vital part of the transformation process.

Everyday living, every situation, every relationship, provides us with an option of how we will use our energy. The choice is for health or disease in relationship. We can choose either extreme, selfishness or altruism. Health comes from neither extreme but from somewhere in the middle, from the self who is both selfish and altruistic and who can choose to respond in relationship. The healthiest choice is to relate out of self, a self with needs that have to be taken care of—not always at this exact moment, but sometime. An adult is willing to modify his or her own needs for the well-being of another. But first, the person must acknowledge needs.

Energy is meant to flow through the self. It achieves unique, human expression only through the individual self, through our acknowledging the self's need for some care and attention. We transform human selfish energy into love energy each time we confront ourselves in relationship and, through acknowledging our neediness, choose to let another in.

Relationships with all others, then, provide us with the constant choice to confront ourselves and our own neediness and to choose to use energy responsibly. A responsible relationship to self suggests we use some of our energy to care for ourselves—to take care of our needs. The reality is that we must live with some unmet needs. However, if we ignore all of our needs, the self will find a way to consume all our energy in a bid for some of our attention. This failure to acknowledge our needs will affect our relationships.

If the individual feels uncared for (the self with needs unacknowledged), people in life will be experienced as an intrusion. Such a person finds it difficult to reach out because the self gets in the way. A man or woman who responds harshly or curtly, for example, may be saying: "You have intruded. I can't pay attention to you because my self is in the way." In such a simple encounter lies the possibility of transforming human energy into love energy. If the person can acknowledge his or her need for attention and, with awareness of that need, choose to give attention to another, growth is possible. The choice is to put self aside for the moment, to acknowledge another in need, and to choose to give away some energy to respond to that need, accepting the reality that in giving energy away, I am also touching my own need. This kind of concrete growth is absolutely dependent on relationships.

The transformation of the self does not happen by wishing or thinking. We have to encounter others and through others come to know ourselves. It is only through another that we are confronted with the self. Without the other, we take our preoccupation with ourselves for granted.

This acknowledgment of human needs, along with a willingness to learn adult ways of fulfilling them, is the key to the good use of energy. We confront our own neediness when another makes demands on us. If we are able to acknowledge our neediness and choose out of it, growth is possible, energy is well used. Sometimes the choice will be for self, sometimes for others. The choice to use energy well is what is important, and energy is meant for relationship.

The self remains the most important starting point for relationship. If one cares for self and relates well with self, accepting one's neediness, other relationships will mirror this care. This full appreciation of self is basic to all other relationships, for our love for others is dependent upon our love for ourselves. We cannot ignore our own person. We cannot leave ourselves outside of life. If we do so, we do harm to ourselves and end by misusing energy.

The wisest investment of our energy is in the quality of relationships, initially with ourselves and then with others. They are the source of energy and the means of transforming energy into love. There are no alternative sources of energy for human beings. To involve oneself in relationship is the absolute ingredient for living out the Christian call to be full of love.

Transforming human energy into love energy is a process, a movement from selfishness to altruism. This movement is possible in every encounter to the extent that individuals choose to use their human energy in life-giving ways. We are so apt to minimize the life that is inherent in daily encounters. Some people restrict growth to the peak moments of life—those special encounters. Others look for that intimate, deep sharing wherein lie love and life. The truth is that some never have those experiences and spend their lives waiting for life in relationships to happen. Consequently, they miss the stuff of life along the way.

Our lives consist of the little encounters and it is in the little exchanges of energy that our growth is to be found. The demands of daily dying to self have a high price: an acceptance of the human self that is constantly in need of transformation. The little encounters, such as a conversation in passing with another, give us a choice between attention and distraction; real listening versus real preoccupation; response versus reaction. To welcome another into our lives is always a possibility and always a challenge. The center of energy to be transformed remains the self, the only conduit of power and ultimately of love. Lives are changed, hope is given, and faith is strengthened when the power of love is present.

We believe that God is actively present in human life. The challenge or call is to discern and respond to God's presence in the area of life that is most demanding of the self—relationships.

It is because of and through one another that we face ourselves and in that confrontation begin the process of becoming full of love. "In directing ourselves ever more completely and loyally towards Him, in striving towards Him with all our strength, we use up all the available energies of our body, with no wastage: we come closer, unerringly and with no danger of losing them, to those we love; we make ourselves fitter to do good around us, to radiate peace and goodness."[2] The reality is that as we become full of love, we ultimately become full of God.

---

2. Pierre Teilhard de Chardin, *The Making of a Mind: Letters from a Soldier Priest (1914-1919)* (New York: Harper and Row, 1961), p. 84.

Marie R. Hofer, Ph.D., is a full-time psychotherapist at the House of Affirmation in Montara, California. She studied at the Arnold T. Janssen College in Holland, received her master's degree at the De La Salle Graduate School in the Philippines, and her doctorate at the California School of Professional Psychology in San Francisco. From 1969 to 1972 Dr. Hofer established and coordinated the counseling and guidance services at Fu Jen Catholic University in Taiwan. She has taught languages in Italy and California. In 1979 Dr. Hofer joined the staff of the House of Affirmation; as a clinical psychologist she has a small private practice in San Francisco.

Birth—Bonding—Body

Marie Hofer

Volumes have been written about relationships, and numerous discussions on television and radio focus on this topic. Assuming that others have consulted *Webster's Seventh New Collegiate Dictionary* to get the definition straight, I have turned for some light to the Teacher Supreme in the Bible; certainly the apostles with their demanding master would have asked for a "golden rule" on this matter. And sure enough they did! Of course, they would not have come right out and said: "What could we do to ever please you?" or "What is it that will get us on better terms with you? We want to be on our best behavior, but the anxiety of not knowing where you are at with us is troublesome." So, one of them took courage and, making it sound good and holy, asked: "Who is the greatest in the kingdom of heaven?" (Matt. 18:1-4). Jesus, calling to himself a child, put this child in the midst of them and told them in no uncertain terms that they were never going to succeed unless they changed and became like children. Then he said something about needing the humility of that child to become truly great and acceptable.

Obviously, this was just one more rule the practical significance of which they did not understand. It was not long after this instruction that children were brought to Jesus, and the apostles began to chase them away in the hope of pleasing their master (Matt. 19:13-15). We know what followed. He rebuked them and gathering the children, bonded with them by blessing them.

It is doubtful that the apostles got the message; it is doubtful we know what relationship is all about. The only helpful clue Jesus gives is the "humility" of children. In all honesty, however, I must say that in my experience with children I have not seen any humility whatsoever; there is not a humble bone in them. As a matter of fact, I think they are incapable of humility, at least as we define it.

Wanting to do a good deed, I recently babysat my friends' children on a Sunday to give them time to be by themselves. The day with these healthy four- and six-year-olds was both exciting and trying. As quickly as the day wore on I wore out, and the children did not hesitate to test my patience. Finally, it came to a scene in the kitchen. Using a hefty stick they poked at everything: drawers, pots, food, me, as I tried to prepare dinner in the midst of all this turmoil. My orders to put the stick away were, of course, in vain. My annoyance grew. So, I grabbed the stick, and in the process accidentally poked the little one. The next thing I saw was the bigger one's fist raised threateningly at me; the little one cried and threw all my apple crisp ingredients on the floor.

That night, exhausted, I prayed: Lord, you could not have said this about children and humility; or if you did, you must have been speaking about the very, very little ones who are not yet spoiled by societal values. I began to search for the answer to the problem of humility by looking at the main difference between the adult and the child, primarily the infant, for whom the intellect is not as yet a complicating factor.

One thing became immediately apparent: babies are very clear about their likes and dislikes. Even before birth they use their bodies to communicate this. A pregnant woman told me the other day about her sleeping difficulties. "The problem is," she said, "that the baby won't let me sleep on my right side as I usually do. It is very definite in what it wants." Mothers report that their fetuses kick in protest about all kinds of matters: loud noises, the mother's fear and anxiety, cold water entering her stomach, or such things as rock music and even Beethoven (Vivaldi and Mozart, by contrast, are their favorite composers). On the other hand, they quiet down if mother's belly is gently stroked or when they are calmly talked to. Fetuses also like sweet stuff. If saccharine is added to their amniotic fluid, their rate of swallowing doubles.[1] What excellent taste, what excellent use of the body to communicate!

Birth has a drama all of its own which changes the symbiotic relationship between mother and child into an interactive one. Although birth is basically supposed to be a pleasurable experience, infants frequently protest mightily, for instance, by a refusal to breathe. The tiny body arches, saying: I don't like to be separate! But newborns are by no means passive in the process of bonding with mother. They are by nature assertive. Crying quickly brings the caretaker, warmth, food, the diaper. If these gifts are agreeable to their needs they calm down and eventually reward the giver by smiling, waving, and crowing. If they are not pleased they will fuss for more, ordering everybody in sight around until the needed something is provided. This initiating behavior and frank communication of needs continues well through infancy. Several years ago *Psychology Today* published an article entitled "Bringing up Mother."[2] The accompanying illustration showed a woman on all fours, harnessed, the child sitting on her back holding the reins—a very telling picture of the power of bodily needs! Infants will generally get along with their caretaker if their bodies are warmly and tenderly fondled, if they are promptly fed and made comfortable. They show pleasure and gratitude by moving toward the source of this goodness. They reward by eye contact, arm movement, gurgling, and later through reaching and holding on. If, on the contrary, infants are unhappy with the caretaker's behavior, they

1. Thomas Verny and John Kelly, *The Secret Life of the Unborn Child* (New York: Summit Books, 1981).

2. Julius Segal and Herbert Yahraes, "Bringing up Mother," *Psychology Today* 12 (November 1978): 90-96.

will show their displeasure by withdrawing their bodies; for the body, a highly sensitive, precise, and creative instrument, is their only source of knowledge and means of communication. A very moving example of this use of the body is the case of little Kristina:

> At birth, Kristina was robust and healthy. Then something strange happened. Bonding babies invariably move toward the maternal breast, but inexplicably, Kristina didn't. Each time her mother's breast was offered, she turned her head away. At first, Peter [Fedor-Freybergh; her doctor] thought she might be ill, but when Kristina devoured a bottle of formula milk in the nursery later, he decided her reaction was a temporary aberration. It wasn't. The next day, when Kristina was brought to her mother's room, she refused her breast again; the same thing happened for several days thereafter.
>
> Concerned, but also curious, Peter devised a clever experiment. He told another patient of his about Kristina's baffling behavior and that woman agreed to try breastfeeding the child. When a sleepy Kristina was placed in her arms by a nurse, instead of spurning the woman's breast as she had her mother's, Kristina grasped it and began sucking for all she was worth. Surprised by her reaction, Peter visited with Kristina's mother the next day and told her what had happened. "Why do you suppose the child reacted that way?" he asked. The woman said she didn't know. "Was there an illness during her [sic] pregnancy, perhaps?" he suggested. "No, none," she replied. Peter then asked, point-blank, "Well, did you want to get pregnant then?" The woman looked up at him and said, "No, I didn't, I wanted an abortion. My husband wanted the child. That's why I had her."[3]

This was news to the doctor but not to little Kristina. She had sensed her mother's rejection long before birth. She was not willing to compromise and so she withdrew. What would most adults do in a similar situation? They would probably be unaware of the warning signals from within, stumble right into the relationship, and only gradually and painfully realize the subtle messages of rejection. Babies are totally dependent on the

---

3. Verny and Kelly, *The Secret Life,* p. 77.

wisdom of their bodies. They are unequivocal in their needs, wants, and likes. The child is body. We too are our bodies; but we may have largely deadened the body's intelligence through fears of intimacy and sexuality, shoulds, false ideals, a need for martyrdom, and so forth. In sum, the only intrinsic difference I found between childness and adultness is in the use of the body.

Coming back to Jesus and his command to be childlike, I therefore conclude he was talking about the need to return to the body as a source of wholenes and holiness. Of course, he himself went through the whole process of conception, birth, infancy, and childhood; as we say, "he humbled himself and became flesh." So, I speculate, this is the kind of humility he was recommending—the body kind.

Take a minute now to experience your body. You may be feeling excitement, peace, boredom, disappointment, whatever. Now locate this feeling in your body. You may be experiencing it as a tingling in your hands, a pleasant sensation in your chest, a slight trembling in your legs, a lump in your throat, or a pain in your neck. When you have located the feeling and the sensation, communicate something caring to that part of your body. Then slowly let go of the experience. You have just meaningfully related to your body, brought together a feeling with a corresponding physical sensation. In addition, you have learned where a certain feeling is housed. It is a good relaxation exercise as well as a way of healing your mind-body split.

Our interactions with others are a constant challenge to be aware of our bodies. Physical reactions to someone can be a pretty clear indicator of whether to pursue a relationship or to pull back. A young man I was seeing in therapy reported feeling attracted to a woman but at the same time quite anxious about the prospect of approaching her. It seemed more than just a normal anxiety over initiating a relationship. He located the anxiety in the middle of his back, as an uncomfortable, heavy pressure. In exploring the problem he became aware that this woman had been frequently and highly spoken of at home, probably, as he later realized, as a suggestion for him to seek her out. He obeyed by becoming vaguely attracted to her. His emotional reaction, however, was symbolized by the pressure in his back: "Get them [his parents] and her off my back!"

We all know about body language and conflicting messages: words may say one thing, the whole demeanor another. For instance, the person who emphatically says "I don't need any help!" but who leans forward, ready to collapse in our arms, is sending a mixed message. It becomes difficult to establish a normal relationship with people who are unclear in their communications. The lack of clarity creates confusion and we feel like pulling away.

Similarly, mind-body splits lead us into setting up failure. When we say no but mean yes, the result can be a catastrophe. The following is a personal example that I am not too proud of: I had a weekend all planned. A friend called and asked me whether I was free to help with his garage sale. I went. It was a disaster. I stumbled over things, fell twice, and broke two dishes and an antique mirror. I was obviously furious, and my hands and legs acted out. I could go on and talk about why it does not further our relationships if we go unconscious and then get under people's skin, hit somebody below the belt, become accident prone, give ourselves headaches and stomach ulcers. The point is that the body speaks whether we like it or not.

Relationships with ourselves, others, and God are redeemable. We can approach this process of healing by treating our needs, wants, desires as the wise child in us, gently guiding them—as a mother guides her body—through the wisdom of our minds. Thus I conclude with a prayer:

You told us Lord, to relate to you in a childlike manner.
I accept and celebrate my body as the child in me
that is wise and good.
It's all I've got.
It contains all of me.
I will rebirth it in its wisdom of relating.
And lastly, Lord, I humbly thank you for my child, the body.